LIFTOFF

THE **SELF-EMPOWERMENT** GUIDE FOR TEENS

3 EASY STEPS TO TURN **NEGATIVE BELIEFS** INTO **POSITIVE ACTIONS**

ILENE SKEEN

First Edition
ISBN-13: 978-1533281401
ISBN-10: 1533281408

hare your story or ask a question at http://liftoff4teens.com.

To hold an unchanging youth is to reach at the end the vision with which one started.

— **Ayn Rand**

Contents

Contents

Introduction

Does stress *overwhelm* you? Doing well in school and planning for college are worries. Learning to drive and getting a job are nerve-wracking.

Are you *anxious* about being accepted? Dating (or not dating), peer pressure, and parental controls are challenging. Wrong decisions about drugs, alcohol, sex, and money are dangerous.

Is your mind sometimes in *turmoil*? Do you need to be able to cope with *multiple demands* from all sides? Do you ever feel you're in a hopeless bind and wonder how you got there?

Do you have problems at home, problems in school, and problems with relationships? If you have a job, do you have problems at work? Do you have problems in front of the mirror?

There can be a lot of pain being a teen. Some of it is physical. Your body changes and your bones can ache, especially the bones of your upper legs. You can have painful cramps and physical imperfections. Your nose, your teeth, your skin can worry you and make you self-conscious.

If some of your pain is self-inflicted, you know you're really scared; you're losing control. You feel you may need professional help, but getting help isn't easy either.

Sometimes, you want to give up and say, "This sucks and it's not my fault!" You want to zone out and watch TV or play video games. But that doesn't solve the problems or get you the answers you need. The problems are still there, and ignoring them only makes them worse.

Is being a teen like you're on a rollercoaster? Some days, you're flying and then—boom—you crash. Why can't life be simple? Just talking to friends, parents, or teachers can be tense when they don't understand.

Many people will advise you that every problem will go away if you ignore it long enough. They say, "This too shall pass." But do you really want to serve a sentence of misery? Or do you want answers?

Do you have little or no idea of what you want to do with your life?

Is your mind a jumble of emotions, facts, needs, and wants? Maybe you sometimes wish you were a little kid again and could crawl into a safe space and hug your favorite toy.

Avoiding problems instead of solving them is a sure way to feel blocked, powerless, overwhelmed, and unhappy. So how do you solve your problems when it seems easier to ignore them?

If you feel like shouting, "I DON'T KNOW! TELL ME ALREADY!" you need to read this book. If you're afraid to shout, *Liftoff* is *really* for you.

THE INCREDIBLE, EASY SOLUTION

Liftoff is a unique and practical guide to empower you from teen to adult. Everything in *Liftoff* is real. No myths. No BS. You'll learn that the answers you've been looking for are really much simpler than you think.

You'll learn the *only proven way* to find and keep a positive attitude. You'll crush your negativity habit and transform your life with positive actions.

You'll learn about Job 1. You'll learn how to deal with multiple demands. You'll learn the three-step method to organize all your tasks, projects, goals, and real paying jobs, especially when you're overwhelmed. You'll know when to do Job 1 and what to do for each of your other jobs, *no matter how many you have*.

You'll learn that many small successes will help to you define your life's purpose and pursue it. All successful adults use this method, but no one teaches it, *until now*.

To do any job well, you need the right tools. You'll harness your natural power to organize your life using:

↗ 2 easy worksheets to crush your negativity habit and replace your negative beliefs with positive actions you can do.

↗ An easy 3-step method to achieve positive results under pressure. Never before presented as a worksheet for teens. Not taught in school.

↗ 2 vital checklists that will help you get the facts and understand what to do and when to do it.

You'll increase your *confidence*, the positive belief that you have what it takes to do a job. Using the tools and following instructions, you'll learn what it takes to rise to the next level and know what to do when you get there.

↗ In Level I, you'll overcome the negative beliefs that limit you. You'll work on jobs you can do alone. You'll organize your jobs into steps and do them.

↗ In Level II, you'll learn about the widespread negative beliefs in our culture. You'll learn to choose the positive. You'll understand when and how to work with friends or groups.

↗ In Level III, you'll learn that the capacity for empowerment is naturally within you. You'll gain self-empowerment from your positive experiences and choices.

What do you get when you make *Liftoff* your guide?

↗ You crush your fears. You solve small problems and learn how to choose and then solve bigger problems.

↗ When you solve bigger problems, you can learn to choose and solve the great problems.

↗ You'll know that happiness comes from living with purpose and working toward a meaningful goal. Whatever the size of the challenges you seek to conquer, you can have an excellent life.

Liftoff will teach you to say goodbye to *maybe*, goodbye to *helpless.* If your goal is to have an excellent life, you really can get the energy and inspiration to change the world.

MY LONG ROAD

How do I know? I've spent nearly seven decades thinking about thinking. At age four, I decided that my mother couldn't read my mind because I couldn't read hers. That is my first memory of introspection, thinking about my own thoughts. Since then, thinking about thinking has been a passion. It also has meant reading philosophy and building on thinking.

I was a willful, bright child. At four and a half, I was excited about school and "growing up." I knew how to read.

The first two days of kindergarten were a screaming chaos. I was one of the only children who didn't cry. However, on the third day of kindergarten, I figured out there was something wrong. Kindergarten was turning happy, playful children, people I knew, into docile robots. I cried, but I couldn't explain why. I was scared of school.

I went to three different schools in first grade. I forgot how to read. I failed the first grade IQ test. They wanted to keep me back, but my mother was formidable. She insisted I go ahead. In second grade, I was ahead of everyone again. I decided to be a teacher. I thought I could fix the school so kids would love it.

By fourth grade, I realized that many children were turning off their minds. They would never again be interested in learning. I was at the top of my class.

I failed the seventh grade IQ test. By fifteen, I knew the schools were hopeless for children who had turned off.

At nineteen, I thought the whole system was broken. I was only one person. What could I do?

I believed someone else would surely fix it. I wanted to survive to see that day. I muddled through. I went into the business world.

I designed people-friendly computer and business systems for thirty years. I devised simple, then complex, and then elaborate systems. I solved problems that people thought unsolvable.

Some problems took longer than others to solve. When I started to think about the basic principles of thinking, that's when I really made progress.

I made even more progress when I studied anthropology. I learned that powerlessness is unnatural in all life forms, including humans. Feelings of powerlessness make us do foolish things to try to gain control.

My nephew, who was bright and shy, got in with the wrong crowd. Egged on by a dare, he killed a man in a robbery. He was nineteen. He's in jail for life.

An acquaintance at work complained that she wanted her college-age son home every night by 7:30. She couldn't trust him. I told her she'd better learn trust quickly; that was an unreasonable curfew for a nineteen-year-old. I told her to give him some space or he would explode.

She was adamant and so was her new husband. Three months later, her son solved their problem. He knifed a judge and went to jail. No more worrying about curfew for him or them.

My own son, Gavin, *rescued me* from a breakdown when I was overwhelmed. He was in high school. One night before dinner, he was alarmed when I desperately complained about my new big job. "Mom," he said, "you've got it all backwards." Then he gave me the three easy steps that organized my life:

"Do Job 1. Set up Job 2. Think about Job 3."

Those three simple steps turned my job around. In Chapter 2, you get the whole story and learn how you can make the three steps work for you.

That conversation with Gavin was over 20 years ago. And until 2015, I was still waiting for someone to fix the broken system I had recognized in 1966. But then, everything changed.

Breaking Out of a Broken System, by Seth and Chandler Bolt inspired me with its can-do attitude and practical ideas. *What if everyone could break out of this broken system to a happy and successful life?*

Finally, I realized that it was up to me. If I could show people that individually they could break out of the boxes that confine them, the system would not be broken. It would be working! The distant bell I heard in my inner mind resounded. My purpose was clear. I would write this book. As an author, I would also be a teacher after all.

MY OUTRAGEOUS PROMISE

I promise that *Liftoff* is the most complete and reality-focused book you'll ever read on practical thinking. If you follow this guide, you'll get the excitement of being alive and the peace of mind of knowing that your life is going in the right direction with you in control.

Read each chapter as if your life depends on it, because it does. Use each tool as if you really want to solve your problems, because you do. You will find your purpose, solve your problems, and share your empowerment with the world.

If your main goal in the world is to help people, you'll understand that you help people best by sharing your empowerment. You'll understand that you share your empowerment by trading it.

You'll understand how not to hurt the people you want to help. And you'll know how to think, because thinking is your tool of survival and that's the tool you need to use to build your best life.

THE ONE GREAT REASON TO READ *LIFTOFF* NOW

Your life can be long or short. Whatever its total length, you know one thing: your time is limited. Every minute that you spend in muddled darkness is one less minute in sunlight. The three easy steps at the core of *Liftoff* will be hard for you to practice at first, but they'll get easier.

What are you waiting for? What's stopping you from CRUSHING your negativity and creating a POSITIVE life? Read this book and move on, move out, move up — *lift off*.

Preface — On the Launch Pad

FOR OUR MISSION TOGETHER, please note the following:

↗ *Liftoff* is about powering yourself from teen to adult. You'll learn the three easy steps. You'll practice them and make them fun. In the process of learning and practicing, you'll conquer your fears and find your goals. You'll learn how to turn many small successes into a lifetime of purpose, achievement, and pride.

↗ Throughout *Liftoff*, I use the term "job" to mean a task, chore, activity, mission, assignment, or real paying job. I call a series of such jobs a *Job Stack*.

↗ The goal of our mission is your *self-empowerment.* Self-empowerment is the conviction that you have the power from within yourself to make your adult life the best life it can be.

LIFTOFF INCLUDES 5 TOOLS

This book has 3 worksheets and 2 checklists. Worksheets are a great tool for learning. Your answers will be about *your life.*

Checklists are a tool for confirming your knowledge. You will see for yourself that you're making progress.

This chapter introduces the two checklists in your toolbox. Using the checklists will speed your progress. You need to use these tools to make them yours. At the end of this chapter you will learn how to do that.

During all these years I've been doing this, my experience with thinking has gone from slight to extensive. Whenever I learned a new principle and applied a method to what I was doing, my thinking and my success improved. I live this method.

In *Liftoff,* the worksheets and checklists will help you succeed.

I can tell you my experiences. I can demonstrate how this method works. I've proven this method to myself because I've made it work in my life. I can't prove it to you.

PROVE IT TO YOURSELF

To live this method, you have to make it yours. Do the worksheets when the instructions tell you to do them.

Thomas Edison, inventor of the light bulb, once said, "Genius is 1% inspiration and 99% perspiration." It took him more than 1,000 tries before he found the material that would make a good filament for a light bulb. When a reporter asked him if he was discouraged, he said that he was happy to eliminate the 1,000 wrong materials, because he was 1,000 materials closer to his goal of finding the right material.

Woody Allen, the filmmaker, famously said, "80% of success is just showing up." My father once met Woody Allen. Dad enjoyed repeating the famous saying, but always ended with his own twist, "80% of success is just showing up, *and the rest is following instructions.*"

Well, in a way, by picking up this book, you've "shown up" at the place you need to be to learn that thinking is easy and growing up can be fun.

> Question: So how do you get 100% success, given Edison's 1% for "inspiration" and Woody Allen's 80% for "just showing up?" What more do you need?

> Answer: You need 19% for "following instructions."

My dad was pretty close!

I promise that if you agree to follow the instructions and answer the questions as fully as you can, you'll see the light. As you work through your real-life problems, you'll gain confidence. Self-empowerment can be yours.

You will prove it to yourself.

When you understand the principles of *Liftoff*, you'll set your goals for your own life. You'll learn how to make your own life instructions and follow them.

MAKE THE BEST USE OF YOUR TIME

If you read *Liftoff* without doing the worksheets, you'll learn about practical thinking and you'll learn a lot about my thinking, but you won't learn anything about your own thinking.

If you want *self*-empowerment, you *must* learn about your *own* thinking.

To learn about your own thinking, resolve right now to do each worksheet when the instructions tell you to do it. Your path to self-empowerment starts with you.

Level I

↗ In *Level I*, you'll overcome the negative beliefs that limit you. You'll work on jobs you can do alone. You'll organize your jobs into steps and do them.

1. Put on Your Big Kid Pants

The best part of being a kid is the fun. The best part of being a grownup is the freedom to control your own life. Sometimes, being a teen is the worst. You're not a kid, no fun. You're not an adult, no freedom. If you could have it all, you would keep the fun and spirit of the kid in you and gain the control and freedom of adulthood.

In the scenario below, you're going to find yourself in a box. The box is a metaphor for everything that bothers you and holds you back. It may be very unpleasant and threatening to find yourself in this box.

It is only a metaphor, but from fear and desperation can come great achievements. The box is the first step toward understanding the natural power of action that you have had within you since the day you were born, because you're human. So be brave. Read on and know that this is the very worst that will befall you in *Liftoff,* and you will beat it. Don't quit now; just *follow instructions.*

Imagine you're in a box. The box is just big enough to hold you. The box hems you in on all sides, above, and below. You don't know how to get out. You don't know how you got into the box. The sides of the box are closing in. The box seems to be getting smaller. No, you're getting larger; you're growing.

The box is your childhood and you're outgrowing it.

You have some wonderful things in the box of your childhood. You have your special memories, good times, times when you jumped for joy. You want to keep the best things of your childhood. If you break out of the box, you could smash your childhood and destroy your life forever. You don't want to do that.

Sometimes, it seems like the box isn't so bad because it protects you against the dangers outside of it. But most of the time, you know you're only fooling yourself if you think you can exchange a little box for a bigger one.

Soon there won't be enough room for you in the box. You feel you have to break out. You don't know how. You have to find a way. You don't know what's holding you back. You're afraid.

The fear you have when you imagine the box is real. And even though you're imagining the box, sometimes it feels like the box is real. You want to break out, but you're not ready.

If you're in the habit of saying *no* to yourself, you're in the box. The first thing we're going to do together is explore your world inside the box.

But before we can do anything together, you have to do something for yourself. When you're afraid to do something for yourself, you need a little positive self-talk to overcome your fears.

Susan, a friend of mine **in her seventies**, has a favorite way of talking to herself when she gets in a dicey situation. She says:

C'mon, Susan, put on your big kid pants and deal with it.

Decades ago, young boys dressed in knickers (short pants) and long stockings. When they reached high school, they dressed in long pants, a sign of adulthood. Nowadays, both girls and boys, young and old, can wear pants or shorts and it doesn't have much meaning. But to Susan, "big kid pants" meant being an adult. So that's the meaning I'd like to convey to you and I hope you convey to yourself.

When your fears block and overwhelm you, you're saying *no* to yourself. When you let negative thinking limit you, be very stern. Be your own parent. Be your own drill sergeant. Be your own spaceship commander.

To get to the next level, you need to know you can rise above your fear. Say **your name** in the blank space.

C'mon, _____, put on your big kid pants and deal with it.

Say it aloud a couple of times. Say it so you can hear it. Say it as many times as you need to say it. Watch yourself say it. Say it in the bathroom in front of the mirror. You're growing up.

C'mon, _____, put on your big kid pants and deal with it.

You're going to learn how to deal with it. You've decided. Shout it.

You don't need to be fearless. You don't need to be stupid and risk everything. But you do need to stop second-guessing yourself and start your journey to the next level.

Here's the kind of negative thinking that happens to you in the box:

> *I can't grow up. My parents still treat me like a kid.*
>
> *I can't grow up this fast. My parents expect too much.*
>
> *I can't do (whatever).*
>
> *I'm not good looking.*
>
> *I'm not smart.*
>
> *I don't have (someone else's) advantages.*
>
> *I can't figure this out.*
>
> *I have no confidence.*
>
> *I'm too timid,* meaning, *I don't have enough confidence.*
>
> *I'm just an average kid,* meaning, *I'm not anyone special.*
>
> *I'm too tired,* meaning, *I don't know how to do this easily.*

When you say no to yourself, your action stops. You're frustrated. You're frozen. If you're a victim of negative beliefs, you don't allow yourself to do the things you'd really like to do.

If you give in to negatives, you can wallow in frustration. You can box yourself up in powerlessness. Eventually, you'll explode, self-destruct, or go flat like a tire with a hole in it.

EMPOWERING BELIEFS ENCOURAGE ACTION

How do you crush your negativity habit? It's the simplest thing in the world: you think of a positive, specific statement that's true about you. The wonderful thing about your positive statement is that it is personally yours. You can act on it and make things happen.

My friend Susan knows what it is to be an adult. She knows that empowerment is the natural state of human life. Empowerment comes from positive thinking.

You're reading this book because you want to grow up whole and healthy. Maybe you want to break out. Maybe you want to take action, but you want to be confident that you can get to the next level. Maybe you want to do something really cool. Then you have to think about what is positive. *There's no other way*.

The strength to rise above your fears is already within you. You have to think about empowering beliefs:

I can grow up.

I can be special.

I can be awesome.

I know this.

I can learn this.

I can do this.

This is what I love, and I can figure out how to write about it.

I can figure out how to earn money from it.

I can sell things to people.

I can invent things that people will want.

I can help people.

If you have a positive attitude, you can take positive actions. Of course, success and confidence are more complicated than just being positive. You know that if you don't feel awesome, you can't just wish yourself into being awesome.

So where do you start? How do you get to awesome?

At the beginning of this chapter, you imagined your box and it felt real. Now you need an idea of the positive. You need to know where the positive starts.

When you know where the positive starts, you'll know two things:

↗ How to turn your negative limiting beliefs into positive empowering beliefs.

↗ How to turn your positive, empowering beliefs into positive actions.

Positive starts with you. Next, do Worksheet #1: Negatives that Limit Me. Prove to yourself that positive starts with you.

Worksheet #1 follows. Make it yours. If you're reluctant, give yourself this order:

C'mon, _____, put on your big kid pants and do Worksheet #1.

WORKSHEET #1: NEGATIVES THAT LIMIT ME

Here are the beginnings of six negative statements:

I can't.... ~~Think~~ Drive	I won't.... listen
I'm not.... ~~positive~~ Patient	I don't.... 2
I am too....* ~~talk~~ negative	I have no.... find 3D Screen t v

*The statement "I am too..." does not seem like a negative, but it is a subtle limiting statement. Reword statements such as "I am too..." or "I am only..." into true negatives. For example, "I'm too timid" becomes "I don't have enough confidence" or "I can't fight this bully."

Write your negatives. Write six or more negative statements about things that bother you and you'd like to change. You need to finish the sentences with specific information.

You can use the same beginning for each of your sentences, mix them up, or make up your own. Your negatives could be concrete and specific, such as "I can't swim." Your negatives could also be complex or vague, "I don't know what I want to do with my life."

If you have more than six, that is great. Write out as many as you can. The more you write out, the more you'll have as raw material for your self-improvement. **The more negatives you write, the more opportunities you'll give yourself for success. Put an asterisk (*) next to the negative that bothers you the most.** Take 5 minutes.

HOW TO TRANSFORM YOUR NEGATIVES INTO POSITIVES

After you have written out your true negatives, transform your negatives to positives using Worksheet #2: Positives I Choose.

Your assignment is to look over your list of negatives that limit you and decide which two of all the negative statements on your list are the **easiest** to break through. Restate each one into a **positive statement**. For example, if you wrote, "I can't drive," the positive might be, "I want to learn to drive."

When you look at all your negative statements, it might not be obvious which two are easiest. In that case, I recommend you restate as many of them as you can until you find two positive statements that you think you could do. Take 5-10 minutes.

Name a "What-to-Do." The final part of this assignment is to transform each positive statement into one or more specific **empowering actions**. You want to write down an action that you can take that would be a step toward your goal. It should be realistic and not yet done. Here are some other points to keep in mind:

↗ Your **What-to-Do should be specific, not general**. It if is too general, it won't guide you to concrete action.

↗ For starting out, your action should be something you can do alone. You can be stuck if other people are unwilling or unable to help.

↗ Later you may find a partner or team to work with on some of your goals.

↗ Your action should not trick anyone, hurt anyone or "borrow" anything without permission.

Here's an example of a positive statement and a specific action:

POSITIVE STATEMENT: I want to learn to drive.

SPECIFIC ACTION: I will read the driving rules for my state.

Write down the easiest and most likely to succeed **specific** action that comes out of your positive statement. This is your What-to-Do. Take 5 minutes.

Make positive thinking your habit. Then the box will never bother you again.

Here are some questions you might have:

Q: Can I make more than one What-to-Do from the same Positive Statement?

A: Yes. Multiple empowering actions can come from the same positive statement. Each What-to-Do should be different. It should not be the same thing written two different ways.

GOOD EXAMPLE FROM THE SAME POSITIVE STATEMENT:

Positive Statement #1: I want to earn money by mowing lawns.

What-to-Do #1A: I want to show Dad I know how to mow the lawn.

What-to-Do #1B: I want to mow a lawn to earn money from a neighbor.

Q: Do I need a What-to-Do #2 if I have two from Positive Statement #1?
A: Yes. You should have at least one specific action from each positive statement.

GOOD EXAMPLE FROM TWO DIFFERENT POSITIVE STATEMENTS:

Positive Statement #1: I want to earn money by mowing lawns.

What-to-Do #1: I want to mow a lawn to earn money from a neighbor.

Positive Statement #2: *I want to learn to drive.*

What-to-Do #2: I can take the written test for a permit in my state.

Q: I wrote out a whole bunch of my negative statements and I transformed each of them to positive statements. Do I need a whole bunch of What-to-Do statements?

A: In general, no. For our starting examples, we will keep things simple.

However, if you did a whole bunch of negative to positive statements that are meaningful to you, that's terrific. Congratulations! When you get going, you're going to take off like a rocket.

If you haven't done so yet, please stop and do Worksheets #1 and #2. I can give you a request. Only you can give yourself the order.

C'mon, _____, put on your big kid pants and do Worksheets #1 and #2.

WORKSHEET # 2: POSITIVES I CHOOSE

Negative Statement #1	Positive Statement #1
I can't drive	I will learn to drive

What-to-Do #1
Pratice driving

Negative Statement #2	Positive Statement #2
I don't have a 3D tv	I want will get a 3D tv

What-to-Do #2
Save up to buy a 3D tv

In this chapter, you learned about the box that limits you with your self-imposed walls of negatives. You learned how to transform negatives into positives. You turned your own negatives into positives. You thought of specific positive actions that you can do. You wrote them down.

Of course, this is not the whole story, but if you've started to think in positives, you're ready for your journey to the next level.

2. Job 1 Is the Job You Can Do Now

Liftoff is about real-life practical thinking. You may think that all thinking is hard. The idea behind *Liftoff* is to make thinking easier for you. As you practice practical thinking, *it will get easier.*

Now that doesn't mean that you won't have to think. If you hope that *Liftoff* is going to make thinking superfluous or unnecessary, you're wrong. If you expect that you're going to be able to achieve your goals and live your dreams without thinking, you're mistaken.

If you didn't do the worksheets, please do them now. You will be wasting your time if you go further without completing Worksheets #1 and #2.

If you did Worksheets #1 and #2, you're ready to understand the method behind *Liftoff.*

Here's the most important thing you'll ever learn about jobs, without exception:

You can only do Job 1. Job 1 is the job you can do now.

I use the term *job* to mean a mission, task, chore, activity, assignment, or real paying job. I call a series of such jobs a Job Stack. You're going to build a Job Stack for yourself. You're going to take your own real-life problems, transform them, and map the positives into the three easy steps.

What you call the jobs in your Job Stack is up to you. Have fun with them. Whether you pursue the Great Lawn Mowing Objective, the New Friend Quest, the I Really Hate Doing Laundry Exercise, the Pursuit of a Good Grade in Math Operation or the Sunday Morning Breakfast Taskforce, make it fun while you keep it positive and real.

The Job Stack is a method of turning thought into action. I'm not the inventor of this method. I just understood the method well enough to practice it as if I were running a machine, and to teach others to do it the same way.

Liftoff is the story of how I got the Job Stack and how deeply I've thought about it. The Job Stack organized me. More correctly, the Job Stack enabled me to organize myself. It benefitted everyone who came in contact with it in the same way.

I was successful in using the Job Stack in my job because I saw that it was a system that I could apply to every job. I also saw that the Job Stack helped me to avoid trouble and helped me think about how to deal with trouble.

JUST WHAT I NEEDED WHEN I WAS FEELING OVERWHELMED

The story started at home one night after work. I had recently received a big promotion in my job and was managing a group of 25 people, mostly technical programmers. They were supporting a user community of about three or four hundred. The user community was demanding and frustrated.

I had so many jobs, tasks, and deadlines on my plate, I just wanted to throw up my hands and quit. I was at the end of my rope and I must have sounded desperate when I vented my complaint to my teenage son, who said, "Mom, you have it all backwards. It doesn't matter how many jobs you have piled up on your plate. The only jobs that matter are the jobs that *you can do.*"

He then gave me the speech that changed my life. What he said is in the italic text (as near as I can reconstruct). How I thought about what he said is in each box under the text:

"First, you have Job 1. Job 1 is the job you can do. It's the job that you know what to do. It's all set up. It's waiting for you to do it. You're ready to do it. You do it. You're done! Finished! Put it on your list of accomplishments."

stupid school shit

Job 1 → Newspaper Deliver

THOUGHT ABOUT, SET UP → DO IT→ **DONE!**

I've thought about this job. I've set it up. I'm ready to do it. I do it. I did it. It's finished. **Hooray for me!**

---

*"Then Job 2 comes along. Job 2 is the job you think about. You figure out what steps you need to do the job. You set up the job so that you can do it, but you don't do it. You leave it. **You don't do it.**"*

Job 2 → *News paper*

THOUGHT ABOUT → SET UP

I've thought about this job. I've set it up so I can do it. **But I don't do it? What is this about?**

"The next job is Job 3. Job 3 is another of the many things to do in life. You think about Job 3, but you don't set up—you only think about how you would set it up if you had the time. You think about what you would do, how you would do it if it were set up. What do you need to do? What do you need to know? How long would it take? What would be the achievement if you finished? What would be the result?"

Help mom

Job 3 → ~~Saving money~~

? → THOUGHT ABOUT ~~Sports~~

I've thought about the job. I've thought about setting up the job. I have not set it up. **Still no action?**

"When you get Job 4, your plate is already full. Now you have overflow, but you're not overwhelmed. Why? Because Job 2 is set up and ready to go. Job 2 is your new Job 1. Do it! Job 3 is the

job you've thought about, but it's not set up yet. Job 3 is your new Job 2. Now is the time to set up Job 2. Set up Job 2. Job 4 is the new Job 3; think about Job 3.

"So this is how you handle overflow: You do Job 1, you set up Job 2 (previously known as Job 3), and you think about Job 4, transforming it into Job 3."

Job 4 → ~~Help Map~~ Sport

Aha! **Job 4 is the trigger for action.** The top space in the stack is empty, since I've already done Job 1. Now the stack moves up. I do the new Job 1, set up the new Job 2, and think about the new Job 3.

"It is very clear; the only job you can do is Job 1. Job 1 is the job you've thought about, the job you've set up, and the job that's ready to be done."

I had only a one-word reply to my son's speech, "Wow." I understood the implications. "This turns projects into a process. It's like a machine." Soon I implemented it in running my group.

Let's recap the components of the Job Stack method:

1. Each job or task has three action parts: think about, set up, and do. I use the words *set up* to mean "get ready but don't do it."

2. Three jobs are in your stack at any time: the top one is ready to go, the middle one is ready to be set up, and the bottom one is ready to think about. The fourth job triggers

the doing of the only job ready for you to do, Job 1. The stack moves up accordingly and the new job goes to the bottom as Job 3 as soon as you set up the new Job 2.

There can actually be multiple Job 2s and Job 3s in your Job Stack, but I'll get to that a bit later.

So what happened when I told this to my group at a big staff meeting? I was smart enough to realize that most people have a hard time dealing with change. Many had real reservations, but others just didn't see the point.

Most people went along—after all, I was the boss. They didn't want to argue. Some people raised good objections.

Here are some of the objections and my answers:

Objection #1. In reality, there are always more than three jobs to do.

Yes, but the only job you can do is Job 1. You can't do the others; you're not ready to do them.

The only job you can set up is Job 2. Why? Because you've already set up Job 1, and you cannot set up Job 3 before you think about it.

The job you really need to think deeply about is Job 3, because you've never thought about it before. You've already thought about the other two jobs.

You want to take the *path of least resistance*, which means the shortest, easiest route between two alternatives. You do each activity (thinking, setup, and doing) for each job in its turn.

Objection #2. After Job 3 becomes Job 2, where will the new Job 3 come from?

It will come from Job 4, the next job that you're ready to think about.

Objection #3. Sometimes, you have to split a job in two.

Yes. That will often happen when you're thinking about a job or setting it up. Then you continue thinking about or setting up one part of the split job. If you can do one part of the job and make the remaining job smaller without hurting the overall goal you want to achieve, do it!

You would be working to maximize your efficiency. It is easier to be efficient than inefficient. The status of the remaining part depends on what you're ready to do after you split one part of the job from the original.

Objection #4. Sometimes you have to combine jobs.

Yes. Sometimes it's very efficient to combine jobs. You find similar tasks, jobs, or goals and you combine them. Now the status of the job depends on what you're ready to do after you combine the jobs.

Objection #5. Isn't there some ambiguity here? When you're setting up something for Job 2, isn't the setting up itself Job 1?

Yes. You're right. There is an ambiguity. Since we stand with the idea that Job 1 is the only job you can do, we use the term "Job 1" in two ways.

Some actions move a job forward, but do not complete the job. Some actions complete a job. For example, if we are setting up Job 2 or thinking about Job 3, we call those tasks or actions Job 1 when we do them. This is easy to understand when you have many steps in Job 2, and they must be coordinated before you can complete the job.

The actual Job 1 is the job that we complete when we do it.

Objection #6. Every job is different. How can this possibly work for every job?

Yes. You're right. Every job is different, but **you are the same**. Your use of your mind can follow the same principle for every job. Can you do a job before you've thought about it? No.

If a job needs setting up, can you do a job before you've set it up? No. (Remember, achievement is always positive. Don't waste your time on the negative. Concentrate on the positive. **Do what you can do.**)

Objection #7. Sometimes, someone demands that you do something you're not ready to do.

Yes. This will happen. The job of a manager is to protect the people doing the actual work from the politics of the people who have unreasonable expectations. If you're not ready, you need to tell me, and you need to have a reason. If it's a good reason, I will fight for you.

Objection #8. What about Job 4? Where does that come from?

Good question! Job 4 comes from the world of jobs labeled 5, the "don't even think about it" jobs. I'll explain this toward the end of our journey, with a really cool revelation how the "don't even think about it" jobs make the Job Stack method into a stupendous empowerment machine.

BENEFITS OF TAKING CONTROL

Finally, I stated the bedrock reason that they would be able to do their jobs better while working for me. I said,

> "You don't have to agree with this method. You don't have to think that it works. I'm not trying to force you to think like I do. But I'm telling you that this is the way I'm going to think about all work from now on.
>
> "When you talk to me about your work, I'm going to ask you, 'What number job are you talking about in terms of my classifications? What thinking have you done? What set up have you done? What remains for you to do?
>
> "'What's your Job 1? How long will it take you to do it? Are you satisfied you have all the answers you need? All the tools that you need? Does the user agree with what you're going to do?'"

They got the point. Fighting over a job that has open questions is pointless. User departments had incentives to finalize their requirements and answer the unanswered questions. The process ran on facts and information, not on wishes, hopes, fears, or needs.

Based on this method, no two jobs would be ready at the same time by the same person. Each job, in its turn, would be ready as soon as the facts and the decisions were clear and complete.

Instead of arguing over bottlenecks, my staff began surprising and delighting users with work flow accomplishments.

Within two weeks, the entire group was using this terminology to discuss their work with me, with each other, and with users. Conversations were fact-based. Requirements were clear.

At that time, the method had no name. It was just a method that worked. People worked individually and cooperatively. They did the jobs that were ready. They organized what wasn't ready. They got the information and the decisions to make them ready. The output was astounding.

One of the members of the group really blossomed with this method. At first, he was a skeptic. Later, he found a better job at another company. When he left, he thanked me for a tremendous work experience. He said he would always remember the fun of the "Skeen Machine."

Now I call this method the Job Stack. The object of the Job Stack is to control the flow of work. You can use the Job Stack to direct your thought processes to be most effective. You can even guide your subconscious thought processes. The Job Stack can also help you manage your emotions, your fears, and your expectations.

Now for you as a teen wanting to grow into an empowered adult, you can adopt the Job Stack method and make it your own:

You don't have to agree with this method. You don't have to think that it works. I'm not trying to force you to think like I do. But I'm telling you that this is the easiest way you'll ever find to think about all your chores, tasks, jobs and goals from now on.

For many years, I didn't have a form. The people of my group and I just did the steps in our heads as best we could. Even so, we sometimes had to write the jobs and steps on a big easel to sort them out.

However, to help you learn and remember the steps, a form will make it easier. In *Liftoff,* the form is Worksheet #3: My Job Stack. Eventually, you'll know how to use the Job Stack so well, you'll do it automatically without using the form.

In Chapter 3, you'll see how the Job Stack works, but first we're going to deal with some unanswered questions in this chapter.

DON'T SKIP STEPS, DON'T STOP NOW

If you've been paying attention, you might have noticed that there's a question mark in the Job 3 space before you can think about it. That question mark is there to indicate that Job 3 is in the flow from Job 4.

Job 4 is the job you're ready to think about next. And where does Job 4 come from? Job 4 comes from Job 5, the infinity of jobs out there. There is so much to do and so much to think about. Job 5 is a jumble. It could be anything from anywhere. You're not ready to think about it.

∞ An infinity of tasks and jobs in the world. You're not ready to think about them. Call each one Job 5 and don't even think about it!	Job 4 → ~~spor~~ ∞ → ? whatever pop~~s~~ Which job or task are you ready to think about next?

WARNING: Before you think deeply about Job 4, you must do the new Job 1!

Of course, in managing your own life, goals, and tasks, you need to be a fair taskmaster and not put unrealistic goals and expectations on yourself. If you are of two or three minds about what you should do next, you're not ready to do anything. When you're not ready to do anything, it means that you don't have a Job 1!

Even though there are only three active jobs in the Job Stack at any one time, don't make the common mistake of thinking that you can only work on a maximum of three jobs at a time. You don't accomplish anything by refusing to do jobs or ignoring the requirements of reality.

The Job Stack is a way of organizing your mind and your jobs for productive, pleasant, and efficient work. The Job Stack relieves pressure. It doesn't add to your pressure or ignore pressure. Deciding which job is Job 1 is entirely up to you and your grasp of your capabilities, interests, and the difficulties of the job.

You may find a new Job 4 that's compelling. You want to do it immediately. You want to make it Job 1. You want it to cut the line! How do you handle that?

Remember, you have Job 2 set up. When you're ready, you can turn it into Job 1 and do it. But you haven't done it, and it will take some time to do it. Remember, you have Job 3, which you've thought about and is ready to be set up. But it's not set up and will take some time to set up. Yet this new Job 4 is compelling and you really want to do it.

Where does it fit in? How much thinking is required before you can set it up? How much thinking is required before you can do it? How much time will it take to do it?

Because the new Job 4 is compelling, you've already made answering these four questions your new Job 1. You have interrupted yourself with this new idea.

Don't second guess yourself; figure out your answers to these questions. Then see how your answers compare with the jobs you've already thought about and the job you have set up.

The beauty of the Job Stack is that you control your job flow by stopping points. A *stopping point* is a convenient place to stop on a journey or pause an activity. When you're on a sight-seeing trip, your stopping points are the sights you want to see and the places you want to stay.

If you're doing a job, but you can't complete the whole job now, you want to find a good stopping point before you leave that activity to do something else.

If you have a 10-step job, some of those steps may be good stopping points, others not. Here's what makes a good stopping point:

- You don't waste the work you've done so far.

- You will be able to pick up where you left off when you come back to the activity.

Your Job 2 and Job 3 are each at a good stopping point. You've thought about Job 2 and set it up, but you haven't done it yet. You've thought about Job 3, but you haven't done it or set it up.

All of your jobs may have time constraints on them that you have to take into account, but it's up to you to decide the job that you'll do now.

What's your path of least resistance? Is it easier and quicker to do this new job than to do Job 2? If yes, do the new job, of course. Is it easier to turn your current Job 2 into Job 1 and do that than it would be to do this new Job 4? Then turn Job 2 into Job 1, of course, and think about how you would set up Job 4, so it could skip the line.

If it's easier to transform Job 3 into Job 2 and then think about this new job, which will be the new Job 3, then that's what you do.

You maintain the excitement, quality, and efficiency of what you accomplish while taking the path of least resistance through thinking, setting up, and choosing which of your jobs is the next Job 1.

As long as you maintain your jobs at good stopping points—doing pieces that you can do and getting ready other pieces by setting them up, the limit to the number of jobs you can personally handle is up to you. That limit will expand as you grow in expertise, confidence, and self-empowerment.

Once you use this system and have good control, you'll probably juggle multiple jobs in the Job 2 and Job 3 categories at the same time. Most productive adults do just that.

You think about Job 3, and maybe everything is resolved except one or two last questions. There's no way to get the answers now, so you set it aside, knowing you can finish thinking when answers are available. That means you can think about something else. If you become stuck on that, you note where you are and then set it aside.

You think about Job 2 and set it up, but you may set it aside. You may be thinking about another Job 3 or setting up another Job 2. That one might need permission or something else that makes it not ready for you to do. This doesn't bring the Job Stack to a halt; it means that you can think about other jobs that interest you.

The fact remains, when you're working actively on any job, your work is Job 1. Whether it's doing it to completion or you're doing a step within a larger job, the step you're doing is always Job 1. While you're working on that job, whether it's in the thinking phase, the setting up phase, or the completion phase, the step that it's in or the phase that it's in is Job 1 while you're doing it.

Thomas Edison told of using a similar method, when a reporter asked Edison if he had come to Florida to rest:

> *"Rest! Why, I have come down here to work harder, if anything. I will tell you how I rest; I am working on at least six or seven ideas. When I get tired of one I switch off onto another and alternate to such an extent that I have a constant succession of new and pleasurable efforts."*[1]

When you create your Job Stack, it's yours. You can make it simple or complex. If it gets too difficult, you can make it simpler. If it gets too easy, you can use it only for harder or more complex jobs. Like Thomas Edison, you can have multiple Job 2s and Job 3s in your Job Stack.

3. Welcome to Job Stack 101

Whether you have one job or a thousand, the three easy steps to turn negative beliefs into positive achievements are the same. First, you must have positive beliefs and positive actions to even think about positive achievements.

Decide on a positive statement and something positive you want to achieve. Since you have completed Worksheets #1 and #2, you have at least four positive items from Chapter 1.

This is how you would think about the three easy steps if you had to do only one job:

Step 1: You would think about the job and get the facts.

Step 2: You would think about the steps and get ready to do the job.

Step 3: You would do the job.

Because teens and adults almost always have more than one job, *Liftoff* shows you how to do *multiple jobs* in an orderly, adult way without getting overwhelmed:

Job 1: You do the job that is ready.

Job 2: You set up the job you've thought about. You get ready to do it.

Job 3: You think about the job and get the facts.

Before you start on your own Job Stack, you can read the example below. You'll see how Brian filled out his Job Stack form based on the entries he made in Worksheet #2. The example is simple, but it has some challenges. Be sure to read the explanation following the form because it will tell you some of the decisions Brian faced. He also faced some setbacks and overcame them.

BRIAN'S JOB STACK

Brian is very excited about two positive things: learning to drive and earning his own money. He has studied the "Rules of the Road" from his state since he was 12 and knows them thoroughly. He took the online tests. Now he's old enough to take the test for real. Brian's dad helped him fill out the form and get the required documents. He also agreed to take Brian over to the DMV. Brian made an appointment to take the test.

When Brian gets his permit, he wants to ask his dad if he could mow the family's lawn. This way, he can prove he's responsible enough to mow neighbors' lawns to earn money for himself.

Here's his example filled out for two positive statements and three what-to-do statements.

BRIAN'S Worksheet #2: Positives I Choose

Positive Statement #1: I want to learn to drive.

What-to-Do #1: I can take the written test for a permit in my state.

Positive Statement #2: I want to earn money by mowing lawns.

What-to-Do #2A: I want to show Dad I know how to mow the lawn.

What-to-Do #2B: I want to mow a lawn to earn money from a neighbor.

JOB 1 → READY TO GO

What-to-Do #1: I can take the written test for a permit for my state. (Prepared, can get to DMV for the test).

JOB 2 → SET UP

What-to-Do #2A: *I want to show Dad I know how to mow the lawn. (Need permission, time)*

What-to-Do #2B: *I want to mow a lawn to earn money from a neighbor. (Need agreement, time)*

JOB 3 → THINK ABOUT

Positive Statement #1: I want to learn to drive. (Next steps)

The specific action, *I can take the written test for a permit for my state*, appears as Job 1. Brian can do that today. Brian's appointment is today. After all the preparation, taking the test is Job 1. The positive statement 1, *I want to learn to drive*, appears here as Job 3. It's not a specific action statement and doesn't fit in any other job category. Brian knows he has to think about the next steps that he needs to take to get his license.

You can see there were actually many steps that Brian took to reach the point of taking the permit test. When he has his permit, it will be a real accomplishment. Yay!

Notice that the second positive statement, "I want to earn money from mowing lawns" is left off the Job Stack. We have two jobs in the Job 2 box. Both require permission and scheduling. Since Brian has two positive related actions based on the same positive statement, he can list them as components of the same job.

Brian is pretty sure he can get the permission and scheduling. He also thinks that his elderly neighbor, Mr. H., would hire him if he saw Brian mowing his own lawn. He knows he needs to think about the next steps for lawn mowing also, but not right now. Thinking about more steps for lawn mowing is Job 4.

Brian's lawn mowing job required Brian to ask his dad for permission and ask a neighbor, Mr. H., about his lawn. The lawn mowing job had multiple steps, so it was a Job 2.

You might think that the actual lawn mowing was the only "work." That would be wrong. Every part of a job is a part of the job, so it's all work if you have to do it to complete the job.

If you think that some of the steps of a job are not work, you'll have a tendency to forget those steps and leave them out. You don't want to do that!

Right now, Brian is concentrating on taking the permit test, Job 1. He's not thinking about the steps of Job 2, mowing his lawn and Mr. H's lawn. He knows he has to think more about the next steps in learning to drive, Job 3, when he gets a chance.

When Brian gets his permit, his Job 1 will be complete. While he's waiting to get it, suddenly he realizes that it would be a good time to set up mowing the family lawn for Saturday. If his dad agrees, Brian will make mowing the family lawn on Saturday his Saturday Job 1.

Brian feels he's in control of his life in these two positive areas even if things don't happen exactly as he hopes. If his dad is busy on Saturday, Brian will go for another day. If Mr. H. won't hire him, Brian will ask another neighbor.

The Job Stack is teaching Brian maturity. He's learning that everything happens in its own time. By taking this mature view, Brian also gets to fully enjoy all the things he makes happen. When you enjoy the things you make happen, you get the energy and enthusiasm to do more.

The Job Stack form is a convenience. It has built-in flexibility. You use the form to help you think about what positive actions you can do next.

YOUR JOB STACK

Now your Job 1 is to complete Worksheet #3: My Job Stack, using your Worksheet #2 from Chapter 1. From Worksheet #2, you have two positive statements and at least two What-to-Do statements. The first thing you want to know is whether there's a Job 1 in your What-to-Do statements.

When you put jobs in your Job Stack, the jobs don't go into the different slots based on your emotional attachment or dislike of any job. **You base the position of the jobs in the Job Stack on the facts of each job and how you need to do it.**

Take a personal look at your What-to-Do statements and decide which (if any) is Job 1. Look over the *Tests for Job 1* below to get an idea of the kind of questions to ask yourself when thinking for success. You want to make sure that you have good reasons to do the job and no reasons not to do it.

Tests for Job 1 – Thinking for Success.

Embrace Positive Reasons and Expectations:

↗ Job 1 is always a job that you can do now.

↗ You can complete it today.

↗ You have time to complete it today.

↗ Job 1 is a job that is a good thing to do.

↗ You'll be better for it in some specific way.

↗ If you've done it before, you know how to do it.

↗ If you're doing the job for the first time, you know what to do in detail.

↗ You'll succeed, or at least, success is likely.

↗ You're ready to do it. Nothing stands in the way of your doing it.

↗ You think you should do it.

↗ You need to decide to do it.

Avoid Negative Outcomes:

↗ No one will be worse for it.

↗ You're not going to hurt anyone if you do it.

↗ You're not going to trick anyone or act maliciously.

↗ You're not going to borrow anything without permission.

↗ You're not going to break the law.

Test each of your What-to-Do statements for your reasons and expectations from the lists above.

If more than one potential Job 1 passes this test, then Job 1 is the easiest. You may have multiple simple jobs you call Job 1. You would do them one at a time, the easiest first.

You may also have more complicated jobs that are Job 2 or Job 3. Checklist #2 in Chapter 5 presents the questions in a slightly different way to help you decide.

You can make notes on Worksheet #2 where you will put each positive statement and What-to-Do (Job 1, 2 or 3). When you are familiar with thinking for success, it will become automatic. You won't need to write everything down because it will be part of your psyche.

Realistically, you may not have a Job 1 in your What-to-Do statements. You're just getting started with this and it's a new mindset.

Your What-to-Do statements may take longer than one day. They may take time to set up, or have other requirements. That's understandable. If you cannot easily create a Job 1 out of your positive statements, don't worry about it. It will get easier with practice.

As you read the next several chapters, you'll learn more about practical thinking, negativity, and Job 1. You may think of a great Job 1 while you're reading. If you do, you can put it in your Job Stack, make sure it passes the Thinking for Success — Tests for Job 1, and then do it.

This adds up to three simple mandates:

1. Success counts.

2. Limiting negatives is important.

3. Good intentions do not count.

Success at positive actions is positive unless there are downsides to your actions. Good intentions do not count. If you intend to do a job and you don't do it, it doesn't count as an accomplishment.

We must be careful not to let our emotions dictate to us which job to do as Job 1. We may *feel* that we want to do a certain job more than another one. In the Job Stack method, emotions are not the tools we use to decide on which job is Job 1.

We may want to let our feelings command our actions. We must make our thinking the commander of our actions.

If something blocks us from acting, and we don't know how to think though our actions to a happy outcome, we can have a tantrum, stamp our feet, hit the wall with a fist, throw a plate, smash a window, lash out destructively, and wind up in jail or worse.

The key to understanding why we don't let our emotions dictate our actions is very simple. Emotions are feelings arising from our current situation and our memories of past experiences in similar situations. We don't want to deny them; we want to understand them.

Emotions tell us to do something or avoid something because the action is *for us* or *against us*. Now that sounds like a good thing, because we want to do actions that are for us and avoid things that are against us. The question is: which particular action should we do now?

Emotions are always about *right now,* yet emotions come from our past evaluations about past events. Emotions do not guarantee that just because we feel something, the action that we *feel* we should do is the right thing to do for us, for now, for where we are, and for what is happening at the moment.

Here's where the idea of limiting negatives can save us from making serious mistakes. We want to act with good reasons when we do things. Good reasons are the hallmark of a happy, healthy adulthood.

Acting on emotions without the benefit of thinking things through and finding good reasons to do what we do, is the hallmark of children, often spoiled children. "Grow up!" their parents shout in frustration, but often, the parents are not a good guide.

Here's the danger. When we have emotions that push us or pull us to act without thinking, we can go down one of four possible paths:

1. We can try to do the action, even if we have no idea of whether or not we would succeed.

    We should reject this path because we want success, not failure.

2. We can block ourselves from doing something without evaluating whether it's the *right* thing to do and *why* it is the right thing to do.

    We should reject this path because it is the path of repression. Repression is the emotional variation of *I can't*, when people allow fear to paralyze them into inaction.

3. We can ask someone else if they think we should do this action, and let their evaluation be our guide.

    We can use this path sparingly only if the person is someone we trust and they give good reasons for their judgments. A good reason arises from facts, not evaluations or opinions *based on emotions*.

We must then take responsibility for agreeing with their reasons. We'll learn more about getting to the facts in Chapter 5.

4. We can think it through for ourselves.

   Yes, this may take longer. Yes, we may make mistakes, but, in the final analysis, we need to make mistakes to learn.

   If something we try works perfectly the first time we try it, we don't know the causes of our success. When we don't know the causes, we can't repeat the action with enough precision to succeed again.

We'll learn more about applying thought to action in the chapters on practical thinking and thinking in principle.

We must say *no* to acting wholly on emotions because emotions are not a reliable guide to action. You'll learn more about the role of emotions in Chapter 13, Mission Control. For now, we're just going to leave this subject with the idea that emotions are not a reason to act unless there's a genuine emergency.

Even in an emergency, emotions may try to compel you to act, but they are not a reason to act or a guide to action. In an emergency, it's clear that your training must take over, not your emotions.

The next challenge is Worksheet #3. If you've found a Job 1, you should have everything you need to enter your positive actions and What-to-Do statements into Worksheet #3. You may want to reread Brian's Job Stack again to get a clearer picture of what he did.

If you have no Job 1 in your What-to-Do statements, you should still fill out the Job Stack with what you have. Don't stress over this. It's a work in progress, and you may be out of your comfort zone, because you don't know whether your entries are right.

You can use the two checklists in Chapter 5. Checklist #1: Clear Thinking will help you understand how to get to the facts of each job you do. Checklist #2: Job Analysis will help you figure out Job 2 and Job 3. If you're relaxed and going with the flow, you'll get to the same place soon anyway.

Worksheet #3 has two sides to fill out. The first side has the large boxes in which you put your three jobs. The instruction side is a condensed version of the **Tests for Job 1** questions you saw earlier in this chapter.

Find any routine, undone task and make it your Job 1.

It's better to put something in your Job Stack as Job 1, than leave it empty. Job 1 is your Do-It-Now Mission. It can be any undone homework assignment or chore that you need to do today. You could also try to find a smaller task within one of your other jobs and make that into the job you can do today.

To keep things simple, your first Job 1 should be something you can do alone. Write this assignment or chore as your Job 1.

On the instruction page after Worksheet #3, review the first 10 questions. If the first eight questions are true, fill in your title for your Job 1 in question nine. Write "alone" in question 10. If you haven't already done so, add your Job 1 to the front of Worksheet #3.

Instead of being stuck, you're taking a positive action to get something meaningful done today and learn how to use the Job Stack. Hooray for you!

In the next chapter, you'll learn that finding your purpose starts with doing Job 1, the job you can do. In Chapter 8, we'll get into a lot of detail on finding Job 1.

Now, if you haven't already done so, fill out as much of Worksheet #3: My Job Stack as you can. After you complete the first ten questions, do your Job 1.

When you are finished with Job 1, go back to complete the form. If your Job 1 worked out great – congratulations!

If not, what went wrong? Was it okay, but less than optimum? Answer honestly and factually. This form is for you to be honest with yourself. How much you get out of the Job Stack method will depend on the honesty you put into it.

Make every Job 1 outcome a learning experience.

WORKSHEET #3: MY JOB STACK

↗ *Job 1 is the job you can do. It is the job that you know what to do. It's all set up and waiting for you to do it. You're ready to do it.*

↗ *Job 2 is the job you think about. You figure out the steps you need to do the job. You set up the job so that you can do it, but you don't do it. You're not ready to do it.*

↗ *Job 3 is the job you think about, but you don't set up -- you only think about how you would set it up if you had the time. What do you need to do?*

What do you need to know? How long it would take? What would be the achievement when you finished the job?

JOB 1 → READY TO GO

Newspaper

JOB 2 → SET UP

Homework

JOB 3 → THINK ABOUT

Help out

INSTRUCTIONS FOR WORKSHEET #3:

When you have Job 1, 2 & 3 filled in, check the first statement in the list below. Then check each statement that is true about you and your Job 1. Write what Job 1 is on line 9. If you have a partner or team, write that information on line 10:

1. ☑ I have a Job 1 on Worksheet #3.
2. ☑ I can start Job 1 today.
3. ☑ I can complete it today.
4. ☑ My Job 1 is good.
5. ☑ My Job 1 will not hurt anyone.
6. ☑ My Job 1 will not trick anyone.
7. ☑ My Job 1 will not "borrow" anything without permission.
8. ☑ I should do my Job 1.
9. ☑ I will do my Job 1: _wednsday_
10. ☐ I am doing my Job 1 with: _He is wagon_

If you have a partner or team, make sure they are ready, too. Go ahead and do your Job 1 now. Come back when you finish it.

If you stopped to do your Job 1 and you did it okay, add a check below:

11. ☑ I did my Job 1 okay. Yay!

If your job was NOT okay, add an x below:

12. ☐ My Job 1 was NOT okay.

Write what happened, good or bad. Be specific and factual (no opinions or evaluations, just the facts).

I deliver newspaper
Then i poep and
fart lol roth x D
_yo)o_

Use Worksheet #2 to transform any negative to positive and find a new positive What-to-Do.
Make this Job 1 outcome a learning experience.

4. Finding Your Purpose

Purpose always answers the question *why*. Why do you do what you do?

We write Purpose (with a capital "P") when we are talking about Life Purpose – the focus of your entire life. Finding your Purpose can be the scariest quest on the planet.

When I started this book, I realized that for many people, Purpose is elusive. Purpose is especially scary if you're a teen. You have no idea of what you should do, would enjoy or be good at. You're not ready to focus your entire life on one Purpose.

Unlike all the other self-help books that I know, *Liftoff* doesn't start with finding your Purpose. Sometimes, that approach can work with adults, especially if they have a deeply neglected purpose that they've thought about for years.

Right now, finding your Purpose is a Job 5. As you saw from the jobs in the Job Stack, there are only three jobs in the Job Stack. Job 5 is out there in the infinity of all the Job 5s on the planet. It's a "*don't even think about it*" job.

Our approach in finding purpose in this book is very simple and based on you, your life and situation. To find purpose, you must break through the negative barriers that block you. It will sound backwards, but our approach will start with success.

We're not talking about capital "S" Success, the big Life Success that you may dream about. We're talking about the everyday successes of getting things done.

Success starts with the job you can do. Job 1 is the job you can do. So start with Job 1 because it's the job you can do. When you start out, that's purpose enough.

Every success is a positive achievement. Do Job 1, and when you finish Job 1, use the three easy steps to find the next job. Knowing that success can help define your purpose makes every job important.

When you do any job, you have two possible results. When you complete a job as planned or better, it is a clear win. Yay for you! It's not only a success, but if it's a big success, you *know* you're at the next level.

But you don't always come out with the results you expect. Sometimes you fall short. Some people say that if you don't succeed, try, try again. Others say, if you don't succeed, try, try again, and then give up.

If at first you don't succeed

Dust yourself off and try again

—Aaliah

You can hear the song by Aaliah at this link: https://youtu.be/6qOnInTJsos.

If you knew a third alternative, would you make it yours? All successful people know that if at first you don't succeed, **you need to change something before you try again.** And here's another thing no one mentions about making a change: when you make a change, you want to make as small a change as possible.

You want to get closer to your goal of success. If you make too big a change, you may change too much and when you still miss the goal, you won't know why. That will get you even further from your goal.

So be **smart and lazy** about it. Try to figure out what was the cause of the problem, and change only that. Then try again. Are you closer to success or further away?

In their book, *Breaking Out of a Broken System,* Seth and Chandler Bolt recount that doing chores and jobs in their family gave them many opportunities for positive achievement. They call these small wins Mini Successes:

> *"We get these chances daily but many of us miss them because they're often disguised as roadblocks. When we look at each roadblock as simply a pain in the you-know-what, we might miss the lesson we have to learn from it. Solving problems and overcoming challenges provides us with the opportunity to learn what not to do in the future and teaches us that we have the ability to move through obstacles."*[2]

When you work on your obstacles this way, you're teaching yourself to analyze and solve your problems. You will learn much more about practical thinking in Chapter 9. Right now, you need to know that turning disappointments into many Mini Successes is the way to find your purpose.

There's one easy way to find your purpose: **Let your success help define your purpose.** Here's the full sequence on your road to self-empowerment, (with thanks to the Bolt brothers for the first four words):

Failure →*Experience*→*Progress*→*Success*→*Purpose*→ **Empowerment**

Consider your commitment to yourself. Think about *what* might work and *how* it might work. Define a new job. Turn your failure into a learning experience. You're ready to move forward in a positive way. Yay again for you! Clearly, a learning experience is also a win.

If you can't do that job right now, you put it aside. Maybe you need to think more about it. Maybe you need setup. Maybe you need help. If you can't do it now, it's not Job 1. Think about what you can do now to move that poor result back into the Job Stack wherever it belongs.

You will do the job again when it becomes Job 1. Eventually you'll get it done, or you'll get something else done to get to the next level.

In the process of doing your jobs and managing your life, you'll have successes. If you're a gamer, you might have a shelf of tokens to celebrate each success.

I have a special vest that I wear in the cold weather. Whenever I do something I'm really proud of, I take a pin from my pin collection and pin it on my vest. When anyone asks, I say, "I work hard. When I do a good job, I give myself a medal. No one else will." People usually laugh. Then when I wear my vest festooned with all kinds of crazy pins, I know what they mean to me, and I enjoy wearing them.

When you give yourself permission to enjoy your successes, it's easier to find your Purpose. As an option, you can keep a journal of your completed jobs. You can find the format for the Job 1 Log in the Appendix.

5. Tools to Get the Facts

The right tools for the right job
—Popular saying

A plumber has tools. A chef has tools. Even reporters have tools.

You use a tool to do a job. The job is the situation.

The plumber uses a wrench to fix a leak. The chef uses a spatula to turn the steak. A reporter uses a checklist to understand the facts well enough to write the story.

A fact is an actual thing or event, independent of anyone's thoughts about it.

When reporters go after news, they look for six factual answers to six basic questions: who, what, where, when, why, and how.

1. **Who** did that?

2. **What** happened?

3. **Where** did it take place?

65

4. **When** did it take place?

5. **Why** did that happen?

6. **How** did that happen?

A reporter writes about what happened, but these questions are good in any situation when you need to get the facts.

This chapter introduces the two checklists in your toolbox. Using the checklists will speed your progress. You need to use these tools to make them yours. At the end of this chapter you will learn how to do that.

About Checklist #1: Clear Thinking

Checklist #1 contains the reporters' questions adapted to the Job Stack.

It organizes the six questions into three sections: Purpose, Context and Action. The sections make the questions easier to remember.

To make this checklist your own, you need to practice using it to think about your problems and solve them. You need understand your goals in terms of why, what, who, where, when and how.

CHECKLIST #1: CLEAR THINKING

For clear thinking, you need to start with the facts.

You ask and answer six basic questions about your task, job, or goal: **why, what, who, where, when,** and **how.**

Here you see the six questions organized and expanded. The three sections, *Purpose, Context and Action*, will help you remember all six questions. Expand the six questions to match your own purpose, context and action.

1. Purpose

a. **Why? Why do this? What result do I want?**

2. Context

a. **What? What is it?** What do I want or need to accomplish?

b. **Who? Who will do this? I? Will I need help?**

c. **Where? Where will the action take place?**

d. **When? When should it start and end?**

3. Action

a. **How?** *Before*: What do I have to do before I start the job?

b. **How?** *During*: What specific actions will complete the job?

Make your answers factual. **Name specific things, characteristics of things and actions.** Use a separate piece of paper or work online. Answer the six questions: **why, what, who, where, when, and how.**

If you wanted to make a cheat sheet to help you remember the essentials of Checklist #1, you could write it like this:

Purpose: why? Context: what, who, where, when? Action: how?

About Checklist #2: Job Analysis

Checklist # 2 is a guide to tell whether a job is a Job 2 or Job 3. If you know that a job will require multiple steps, it is still a Job 3, until you know why you are doing the job and what you want to accomplish. You also need to know *why* and *what* for each step.

If you know those answers, and you're ready to set up all or some of the steps, the steps that you are ready to set up are your Job 2.

CHECKLIST #2: JOB ANALYSIS

---

1. Job 3 is the job you need to think about.

a. If you do not know WHY you are doing this job, it is a Job 3.

b. If you are not clear on the consequences of this job, it is a Job 3.

2. Job 2 is the job you've thought about. You need to set it up.

a. **Priority:** If you must do other jobs before you can do this job, it is a Job 2.

b. **Arrangements:** If you must ask permission of someone or travel somewhere, it is a Job 2.

c. **Time Constraints**
   i. If you cannot do this job completely in the time you have allotted to do it today, it is a Job 2. You need to make the job smaller, or allow more time.
   ii. If this job will result in a mess when you do it, and you do not have the time to clean up the mess today after you do the job, it is a Job 2.
   iii. You need to get help, make the job smaller, or have more time available. If necessary, break the job into two or more tasks (jobs within jobs).

3. Job 1 is the job you have made ready to do.

a. I am ready and able to do the job.

b. I arranged for traveling.

c. I obtained any permissions.

COMPLETING LEVEL I

We are coming to the end of Level I. Here's what I said you would do in Level I:

↗ In *Level I*, you'll overcome the negative beliefs that limit you. You'll work on jobs you can do alone. You'll organize your jobs into steps and do them.

You've learned a lot. You've used or learned about all five tools in your toolbox. But before we say congratulations, you need to demonstrate *to yourself* that you've learned the information and tools of Level I well enough to get the most out of Level II when you get there.

Let's have a quick review of what you've learned so far:

↗ In Chapter 1, you faced your negatives and turned at least two of them to positives. You thought of a specific positive action that you would like to do. You learned to give yourself stern orders when you needed to:

C'mon, _____, put on your big kid pants and deal with it.

↗ In Chapters 2 and 3, you learned about the Job Stack, set up your first Job Stack form and did one Job 1. You learned the most important truth about jobs:

You can only do Job 1. Job 1 is the job you can do now.

↗ In Chapter 4, you learned that small successes fuel larger successes and success helps you find your purpose. You learned the empowerment sequence:

Failure⟶ *Experience*⟶ *Progress*⟶ *Success*⟶
Purpose⟶ *Empowerment*

↗ In Chapter 5, you learned about the two checklists, *but you haven't used them.*

Here's what I said you will do in Level II:

↗ In *Level II*, you'll learn about the widespread negative beliefs in our culture. You'll learn to choose the positive. You'll understand when and how to work with friends or groups.

I bet it's no surprise to you when I tell you that to get to Level II, *and know you belong there*, you're going to learn to use the two checklists right now! I'm going to show you *how* by giving you an assignment that uses the checklists and guidelines for completing the assignment.

Don't let this daunt you. I'm going to use the six questions of Checklist #1 to form the instructions for this assignment. Just follow these instructions along with me and you'll be fine.

Let's repeat the six essential questions from Checklist #1 to get our bearings:

Purpose: why? Context: what, who, where, when? Action: how?

Next, we'll ask and answer the questions:

Why? Why should you want to learn the checklists well?

By learning to use the two checklists, your understanding will increase and your familiarity with all the tools in your toolbox will improve.

Doing this exercise using your own problems and goals will make the tools real and useful for you. It will also solve some of your problems and get you closer to your goals.

You'll demonstrate two important behaviors: *self-direction* and *self-discipline*. Self-direction means that you give yourself instructions. Self-discipline means that you make sure you carry out your own instructions. When you complete this assignment successfully, you'll be rightly proud.

What? What should you do? Here are guidelines you should use to decide what *you will do*:

Your assignment is to complete five jobs you can do alone over five days. Count the Job 1 you did in Chapter 3 *only* if you need to redo that job because the outcome wasn't okay. For your multiple step jobs, even if you don't complete them, you're going to move them forward in some way over the five days by completing at least one step in each.

If you've been following instructions, you did your first Job 1 in Chapter 3. If you were successful, Job 1 is complete. You need a new Job 1 for your Job Stack worksheet (Worksheet #3). Your new Job 1 may come from a step in Job 2 that you have made ready to do.

You're going to decide exactly what jobs you are going to do in this limited period based on your life, your problems and your goals.

↗ At least two of the jobs should have multiple steps.

↗ You can include the jobs you've already set up in your Job Stack but haven't done.

↗ You can include other jobs by using other negatives from Worksheet #1 and transforming them on Worksheet #2.

↗ If none of those are easy enough to do in 5 days, look for easier ones.

↗ If you are short of Job 1 jobs, you can add some routine jobs like homework, chores, etc.

Who? Will you do this alone? Aside from getting permissions or information from others, you're going to do the jobs in this assignment by yourself.

Where? This section will contain your answer based on each job you select. Some jobs you may do at home, at school or some other place. If there are transportation issues, you should note them.

When? This section will contain your answer based on the time you judge it'll take you to do each job, when you'll start and when you estimate you'll finish.

How? The fastest way to learn how to use Checklist #1 is to write the six essential questions at the top of a page and answer them in writing. Soon Checklist #1 will be yours. On Checklist #1, the "*How*" has two entries: "*Before*" and "*During.*" We need to use them both for these instructions.

You may be thinking now, I can't do this! I can't write all this stuff out! Adults don't do this!

You are correct on the last point. Adults don't write things out, and rest assured, once you learn these tools, you won't need to write things out either! You'll *know* how the tools work.

Most adults have no set method or system. They learned to do what they do through trial and error, without any specific guide. You don't know what trials they went through or mistakes they made to learn what they know the hard way.

Except for the most successful of them, adults just think about what they need to do in their heads as best they can. Some are better at managing their lives than others. They make To-Do lists when they need to. Some, like reporters, may have a mental checklist. Some never learn.

You have the huge advantage of being young enough to learn this method now, in a systematic way, and make it your own.

In Level II, you'll do everything in your head, except for the jobs you will not be doing alone. For those jobs, especially if they are complicated, you'll *want* to make a list of who will do what. That's not a big deal.

In both Levels II and III, you will concentrate on substance instead of methodology.

Here are the **Actions** guidelines for how you'll do your five jobs following Checklist #1:

How? Before:

↗ On a clean sheet of paper write out the six essential questions from Checklist #1 on the top of the page: "Purpose: why? Context: what, who, where, when? Action: how?" Write the job or step as it appears on your the Job Stack form or Worksheet #2. Write the date if you want to keep your notes (good idea).

↗ For each of the jobs or each step in a multiple step job on your Job Stack form, use Checklist #1, Clear Thinking to answer each of the six essential questions.

↗ Next, for the jobs and steps you've just written out, use Checklist #2, Job Analysis, to see that you've classified each job in the right place.

You're going to do five jobs. There are only three boxes on Worksheet #3, My Job Stack. That means that at least one box (Job 1, 2 or 3) will have more than one entry.

It's easy to become confused when you have to move jobs in your Job Stack so that Job 2 becomes Job 1 and Job 3 becomes Job 2, etc. In addition, circumstances may have changed, so that you might really want to re-evaluate the sequence of the jobs. For clarity, start a new Job Stack (Worksheet #3).

To re-evaluate the sequence, ask yourself the three questions which are the essential questions of Checklist #2: Job Analysis:

↗ What do I need to think more about? That's a Job 3.

↗ What do I still need to set up? That's a Job 2.

↗ What can I do now? That's a Job 1.

Put any multiple entries for a Job Stack box in order within that box, easiest first. It's your life, it's your Job Stack. You control the flow.

Please fix this idea firmly in your mind: the point of this assignment is to learn how to use the tools in the *Liftoff* toolbox. You are not going to solve all of your life's problems in five days.

How? During:

↗ Stand up. Take a deep breath. Exhale slowly.

↗ Now, it's up to you.

C'mon, _____, put on your big kid pants and deal with 5 jobs over 5 days. You can do it!

Do your jobs. Pace yourself. Keep a Job 1 Log. Celebrate your successes. Learn from your experience.

Of course, you can just turn the page and start Level II without doing anything further. If you do that, do you really think you're doing yourself a service? I don't, but I'll never know. You might be forty before you figure it out.

Level II

↗ In Level II, you'll learn about the widespread negative beliefs in our culture. You'll learn to choose the positive. You'll understand when and how to work with friends or groups.

Welcome to Level II. I hope you agree that you're making progress.

If Level II had a title, it would be, "How to recognize the broken system and keep it from ruining your life."

6. Limiting Negativity

Negativity is like salt. A little is the spice of life, too much is poison.

Thinking is a process. Humans use thinking to learn how to survive and thrive in the world. In this chapter, you'll learn how to recognize common mistakes that make thinking difficult. By far, the biggest common mistake is negativity.

In Chapter 1, you imagined you were in a box. You made the box from your negative beliefs in your own abilities. Positive thinking was the key to breaking out of the box.

In this chapter, you'll learn that when you limit negativity, thinking *can be easy*.

JANIE'S STOP AND GO STORY

No by itself is unlimited. It is a stop, period—a stop with no end. A stop sign is also a stop, but it is *limited*. A stop sign tells you not to cross the intersection *until you know traffic conditions are safe for you to cross it.* The road is real, the car is real, and the traffic is real. The stop sign is a warning for everyone on the street. If you're walking across the street and you ignore the traffic and the stop sign, you can get really hurt, or worse.

The driver who ignores the stop sign can hit you if he's going too fast and doesn't see you in time. It would be wrong for him to ignore the stop sign, but certainly, it would be worse for you if you were injured or killed.

When would it be safest to cross the intersection? It would be safest when there was no traffic or when the traffic crossing your path stopped at a stop sign or red light.

Here we see a different use of the word *no.* Instead of standing for "don't act," the words *no traffic* in this context describes a limited negative.

We're using this simple story of Janie and her parents so you can see what a difficult time parents can have even with a two-year-old. Learning to understand this simple situation from both sides will help you understand how to communicate in your own, more complex situations.

Janie's mom and dad know that Janie is too young to cross any street by herself. She's not old enough to pay careful attention to the traffic. She doesn't know yet that if she ran into the street, an oncoming car or truck might not be able to stop in time and could hit her.

Janie's mom and dad think they have a simple rule. "We always hold hands and wait until there's no traffic," they say. On a side street, they wait for "no traffic" until they cross. On a busy street, they wait for the light and until the traffic going across their path stops.

This may sound reasonable to you because you know how to cross a street. You know about traffic and you know about accidents, and you might even know a two-year-old who would run into traffic.

To two-year-old Janie, it's not reasonable. She doesn't understand "no traffic." She doesn't know what "traffic" is, so she doesn't have any clue what "no traffic" is. She doesn't get what holding hands has to do with crossing a street.

She knows cars and trucks are big and go fast. Janie doesn't know that fast cars and trucks take time and distance to come to a stop. She doesn't get the idea that crossing the street can be dangerous.

In other words, Janie is like I was! She thinks her parents are just saying "no" again to be bossy and she wants to rebel. Suddenly, she wants to run into the street, just to see if her parents really mean "no" this time.

When Janie jumps off the curb into the street, her father grabs her and pulls her back hard. He's angry and yells, "NO, NO!" Her mother says, "Bad girl! Bad girl!" Janie starts to cry. She's confused and distressed. She still doesn't know what "no traffic" means or what holding hands has to do with anything. She does know that "bad girl" and angry voices are signs that Mom and Dad are angry. Janie wants her parents to like her all the time, but sometimes they make it very hard. Janie's crying ends with a little whimper and she looks up at her parents through her tears. Suddenly, they understand.

Janie's dad takes out his big yellow handkerchief and dries her eyes. Janie's mom bends down and picks her up so that their three faces are all on the same level. "Let's take the time to start over," Janie's mom says to her dad. He nods in agreement.

"Janie," Dad says, "Look at the street. Do you see the cars and trucks going very fast?" Janie nods.

"We want to teach you the safe way to cross the street. Would you like that? You don't want to get hurt, right?" Janie nods again.

"Janie," Mom says, "We don't want you to get hurt either." She gives Janie a hug and Janie gives her a hug back.

"I'm going to put you down so you stand on your own feet now. We'll all hold hands. Daddy will hold one hand and I'll hold the other. Then we'll wait until it's safe and cross the street together. We'll teach you, so that you know when it's safe, too. When you're a big girl, and you know how to do it, you'll be able to cross the street by yourself." They do that.

Notice that the parents' overriding concern is still negative, "We don't want you to get hurt...." However, every action in this plan is entirely positive: Janie will be walking with them, holding hands with them. They'll all wait. They'll teach Janie what she needs to know. She'll learn that moving cars, trucks, buses, fire engines, and even bicycles are "traffic."

Janie will learn to understand that the word "no" used before any *something* means the absence of that *something*. She'll learn how to look for cars right and left. When she knows it, and she can show that she knows it, she'll be able to cross by herself. Janie thinks that life is pretty good now, and Janie's parents feel good, too.

By this example, we see that although "no" is a stop, positive actions promote learning. When learning takes place, the positive actions will change to continue the learning. For example, Janie will learn to look both ways, and her parents will be proud.

As she grows, Janie will learn many more lessons at home and school. She'll become more responsible. She'll enjoy more independence. As Janie learns the habit of positive actions, she'll fuel her own learning and demonstrate maturity.

Janie doesn't have the vocabulary or life experience that you do. She doesn't know how to negotiate. All she can do is whimper. She hasn't lived long enough to suggest a positive alternative. On the other hand, her parents can't read minds.

Your parents don't know why you think the way you do either. They may not be able to do the best job at raising you, but that's exactly where you come in.

As a teen, your own situation is far more complex, but you have many more options. If you're in a situation where your parents "lay down the law," you need to understand their point of view. You could rebel or you could negotiate. If you just rebel, you're not being constructive—you may as well yell, cry, or whimper like two-year-old Janie.

If you're going to negotiate, you need to know your parents' purpose. There must be something deeper than "because I say so." That didn't even work for two-year-old Janie. It certainly won't work for you. Ask for a real reason, but remember, it may be even more difficult for them than for you to face reality.

Be firm but patient. Be kind—they usually love you more than you can even imagine. Win their admiration by granting them the respect of dealing with them not as child to parent, but as one adult to another.

TRUE LIMITING BELIEFS ABOUT THE WORLD

Some negative, limiting beliefs about the world are true. For example, you, as a human, really can't fly without wings, without an airplane or, at the very least, a mechanical lifting device. You can jump off the roof, but you're not going to be able to fly, unless you have a special contraption.

For thousands of years, people wondered about flying. They saw that birds teach their young to fly. They saw all kinds of insects flying.

Hundreds of years ago, many people dismissed the idea of humans flying as against God and nature, but many others all over the world were intrigued. "Why can't we fly?" they asked. "Because you can't," was the answer. True limiting beliefs stopped those people from going further.

The people who were not content with the negative persisted. Finally, they started to ask a positive question:

How do birds fly?

Some people imagined that if they looked like birds and had wings like birds, they would be able to fly like birds. People dressed themselves in feathers and jumped off towers to their deaths.

Finally, the questions became specific:

↗ What facts of nature make flying possible for birds?

Of course, there were many more questions:

↗ What causes hot air to rise and cold air to fall?

↗ Since big birds have bigger wings and little birds have little wings, is there a proportion of weight to wingspan that makes bird flight possible?

As people learned more facts, they had even more questions about how these facts all fit together. People made models and did tests. Many tests didn't work as expected. There were many crashes. But the knowledge of what worked and what didn't work continued to grow. Small successes meant more confirmed answers. Many small successes led to more elaborate tests.

Two key effects form the basis of all flight. The movement of the air over the wings creates the lifting force. The speed of the bird (or plane) pushes it through the air horizontally. Hot air and lighter-than-air gases were good suppliers of lift for balloons, but bulk of the balloon and relatively small engines made the forward speed too slow to get most people excited.

People didn't get the answers overnight, but today, air travel is routine. Airplanes fly people and packages from place to place all over the world.

"The history of aviation has extended over more than two thousand years, from the earliest forms of aviation — kites, and attempts at tower jumping— to supersonic and hypersonic flight by powered, heavier-than-air jets....

"According to the Smithsonian Institution and Fédération Aéronautique Internationale (FAI), the Wright brothers, Orville and Wilbur, made the first sustained, controlled, powered heavier-than-air manned flight at Kill Devil Hills, North Carolina, four miles (8 km) south of Kitty Hawk, North Carolina on December 17, 1903.

"The first flight by Orville Wright, of 120 feet (37 m) in 12 seconds, was recorded in a famous photograph. In the fourth flight of the same day, Wilbur Wright flew 852 feet (260 m) in 59 seconds. The flights were witnessed by three coastal lifesaving crewmembers, a local businessperson, and a boy from the village, making these the first public flights and the first well-documented ones." [3]

Using the principles of motion adapted to the problem of flying, people have learned to body glide at high altitudes. Some extreme sports involve variations of flying, or using skis, snowboards, skateboards, and parachutes to perform tricks and jumps that earlier generations could only imagine.

Thus, in this second common thinking mistake, we see that true limiting beliefs are another form of negativity. Just as Janie and her parents conquered the learning-to-cross-the-street problem when they switched to their positive action plan, the Wright brothers provided the path to achieve air travel when they started to ask specific questions and then test and apply their results. Their breakthrough excited the entire world, and the whole world is better for it.

7. Negatives Everywhere

In the last chapter, we reviewed two common thinking mistakes, negativity as applied to a stop or an absence, and true limiting beliefs, which you've learned are also a form of negativity. And you've learned that in both cases, to counter negativity, you need two things: a positive belief and a specific positive action to test, learn, and confirm the positive belief.

The list of other common mistakes in thinking is long. It would be confusing if you had to remember each of the mistakes separately. The truth is that every single common mistake in thinking is a variation of negativity. Since the principle of countering negativity is always the same (positive belief, positive action plan), you don't have to memorize anything! All you have to do is recognize that the statement or idea is negative—then you know what to do.

Here are six of the most important common thinking mistakes. You'll see how each mistake represents a variation of negativity. Once you read and understand them, I think you'll be astonished how often you hear them in conversations and speeches everywhere.

MISTAKE #1. EMOTIONS OVERRIDING FACTS

↗ I **love** this; it **can't** be **bad**. I **hate** this; it **can't** be **good**.

To know why acting on your emotions is a problem, you need to know the function of emotions. Your emotions are the mental records of your body's physical reaction to pleasure and pain. Your emotions tell you if the experience is "for you" or "against you." When you experience an emotion, you store the feeling and you also store the facts of the situation in your memory.

For example, let's take a good experience. When Janie was around 18 months old, she had a great new experience. She ate ice cream. It was cold and tasty. It was fun to eat. Then every time she heard the words "ice cream," she would be happy. She probably didn't remember the very first time she ate ice cream, but the thought of ice cream made her happy.

Simple emotions are one-sided: all good or all bad. Sometimes emotions are conflicting. Janie likes ice cream very much. One day Janie ate too much ice cream. She ate it very fast. She got a stomachache. Stomachaches are unpleasant. After that, the thought of ice cream was not so happy as before. Janie still likes ice cream because it's tasty and fun to eat. Yet, Janie doesn't like ice cream because it causes stomachaches.

When something is both good and bad and our thinking stops, we're in a muddle. If Janie figures out that the bad part of her ice cream experience is eating it too fast or eating too much, she can still enjoy ice cream and avoid stomachaches. Janie's mother may tell her to eat more slowly. Probably Janie will try that, since she likes ice cream and wants to be able to enjoy it without the stomachache.

If you have memories of a similar event, the memories can heighten the emotion, making it stronger. You often remember your feelings well. Many times, you don't remember the facts of the memory well. It's important to go by current, specific facts, because acting on emotions based on previous facts can lead you to improper actions.

MISTAKE #2. THE CLAIM OF A DIFFERENT REALITY

↗ What's true for you is **not** true for me.

The claim of a different reality is ambiguous. The speaker may be talking only about the mind. On the other hand, the speaker may be talking about the mind and everything we observe in the world.

People who say that things may be true for you but not for them are usually talking only about the mind, such as their emotions or memories. Of course, we all have different emotions and memories. If the speaker is talking only about the mind, the statement is unremarkable.

However, many people promote the philosophy of Immanuel Kant (1724-1804). Kant wrote extensively about reason, the mind and reality. Kant claimed that humans are *incapable* of knowing true reality because we cannot know the "thing-in-itself."[4]

According to Kant, humans are blind to reality and truth. Each person's grasp of reality is subjective and unprovable.

Kant's claim attempts to make people doubt their ability to survive in the world. When people are convinced that their mind is not the key to their own survival, they cease to be individual thinkers. They become like the children of my kindergarten — obedient robots.

The speaker may claim to speak for an entire group:

↗ What's true for some people is **not** true for others.

Active minds are individual and different; they agree based on facts in the world. In this case, you can only conclude that the speaker is speaking for a group of obedient robots.

The issue for you as a teen is your grasp of the objective world, the reality your mind observes every day of your life. You must reject ambiguity and affirm your mind.

Your mind is your tool to understand the world. Your self-empowerment depends on it.

MISTAKE #3. LACK OF CONFIDENCE

↗ I'm **not** sure I will succeed. I **don't** want to **fail**.

Lack of confidence is very distressing because it saps your self-esteem and freezes you. When you concentrate on positive actions and Job 1, you maximize your success percentages and turn what's not an outright success into a learning experience.

MISTAKE #4. DON'T THINK OR ELSE

The reasonable adult teaches you that initiation of force is wrong. If you initiate force, someone should use force to stop you and punish you. That would be justice. The unreasonable adult teaches you that if you're a victim of force, that's only in your mind. You should forgive your attacker. You should show mercy. Mercy is forgiveness without punishment. To deny justice is to commit injustice. The unreasonable adult confuses justice and injustice by telling you they are equal or that mercy is superior.

Might Makes Right:

*You'd better do what I tell you to do or else you **won't** like what I'll do to you. I **don't** have to give you a reason. You **don't** have to think; you just have to obey.*

The bully in the schoolyard beats you up. The adult tyrant makes a system to take your property and put you in jail or kill you if you disagree.

The reasonable adult knows that mercy can be superior to justice only when a law itself is unjust. It's wrong to punish someone for breaking an unjust law. When the law is wrong, mercy for the lawbreaker is justified. The solution for wrong laws is to make the laws right. The job of the law is only to punish actions that initiate force. The job of the law is to serve justice.

MISTAKE #5. MAJOR LOGICAL FALLACIES

Fallacies are errors in thinking. The major logical fallacies occur so often, they have names.

The Fallacy of numbers

*Everyone agrees (on something); they **can't** all be wrong.*

Until Galileo (1564-1642), most people thought the sun revolved around the Earth. All of them were wrong.

91

The Argument from Authority

*The highest authorities say (something). They must know. They **don't** need to explain their reasons. In addition, ordinary people **don't** need to understand or agree with their reasons.*

Until Galileo, the highest authorities thought the sun revolved around the Earth. All of them were wrong. The Inquisition burned people at the stake for disagreeing. The pope placed Galileo under house arrest for the last 8 years of his life. The Earth continued on its path around the sun.

Ad hominem (Argument against the Man)

*You **can't** be right because you're just a kid (or old, rich, poor, female, prejudiced, talk too fast, or a nasty person).*

Probably, ad hominem is the most widely used of all fallacies. The opponent attempts to discredit the argument by attacking the character or situation of the person advancing the argument, instead of confining the conversation to the logic and truth value of the statement.

Begging the question

*You **can't** prove that reality exists. You **can't** prove that you exist.*

To beg the question is to assume the point at issue.

In this case, the speaker claims that proof of reality is both necessary and impossible. However, proof as a concept depends on reality being real and facts being facts. Your proof of reality depends on your existence in reality, or who would be doing the proving?

We prove our logic, our understanding of one fact in relation to another

We do not prove the facts. Facts simply are.

Our apprehension of facts is through our senses. We prove our understanding of facts by surviving and thriving.

Attempt to prove a negative

*You **can't** prove that God **doesn't** exist.*

Only reality exists. We can prove a presence or fail to prove a presence. We can demonstrate an absence only if the something which is absent has positive physical characteristics that we can show to be somewhere else at the time in question.

Circular reasoning

*God created the world from the Void (**nothing**). The evidence of the world is all around us. The evidence of the world is evidence of God.*

God is a being with no form, shape, or substance. People must accept the existence of God on faith, without evidence. Therefore, the world and all of the world's creatures cannot be his creation because everything comes from something. *Nothing* is an absence. An absence cannot produce a something. You may still want to believe in God for reasons of your own—your emotions, your upbringing. That's fine. You just need to be aware that reality is what it is, regardless of your own particular belief system. If you believe in God, you take that belief on faith. Evidence and proof are irrelevant to your belief in God.

MISTAKE #6. CLAIM OF CONTRADICTION

A contradiction is a statement that cannot possibly be true, but the speaker or writer is saying that it is true. The claim of contradiction is the most important negativity mistake because it hides a negative within a positive. The hidden negative stops you even when you don't know it is there.

The claim of contradiction must contain at least one false statement or one statement that is true only *speaking loosely*. Speaking loosely means using a *figure of speech*, not actual fact. When the speaker explains, you know which part of the original statement is actual fact and which part is not actual fact.

Here is a simple example.

Right now, Johnny is at home and at school.

That sounds like a contradiction. Can Johnny really be in two places at once? Of course not.

Here are some possible explanations of this sentence:

↗ If Johnny is at home, then right now, Johnny is at home and **not** at school.

↗ If Johnny is at school, then right now, Johnny is **not** at home; he is at school.

↗ If Johnny is home-schooled, then right now, Johnny is at home while his home-school teacher gives him his lessons. School refers to a place where learning happens, **not** a school building. School, in this explanation is a *figure of speech*.

⬈ If Johnny lives at a boarding school, then right now, Johnny is at his boarding school getting lessons. When Johnny goes for a walk or to another school, he thinks of his school as home. Home refers to a place Johnny returns to regularly, **not** his normal home. Home, in this explanation, is a *figure of speech.*

⬈ If Johnny has been ill a long time, he may be neither at his normal home nor in his normal school. Right now, Johnny thinks of his hospital as home. So he is at home (in the hospital) today, and **not** in his normal home.

⬈ Also, he is able to "attend" his classes via computer, so he thinks of himself at school even though he is **not** at his normal school. Both home and school in this explanation, are figures of speech.

In explanations #1 and 2 above, we learn that Johnny is in one place and not the other.

In explanation #3, we learn that in fact, Johnny is at home. Since he has lessons at home, we can think about him as being in school, even without the school building.

In explanation #4, we learn that in fact, Johnny is in school. Since he is boarding there, we can think about him as being at a temporary "home" when he is there.

In the final explanation, we learn that in fact, Johnny is in a hospital, which is neither a home nor a school. So both parts of the statement are false in fact.

However, we can think about Johnny as being in school while at his temporary home, the hospital.

If you wanted to see Johnny in person, where would you look? At home? At school? At a boarding school? In a hospital? Knowing where Johnny is right now would limit the places you have to go to in order to see him in person. You would want further information before you started out! The limiting negatives would save you time if the speaker hadn't hidden them from you.

Why is this important?

In physical reality, we have to decide to do one thing or another. If a statement is contradictory and both parts are supposed to be true, what do we do? We need to get the reasons, the explanation of why the speaker says both parts are true.

The claim of contradiction is important to understand because contradictions are always impossible *in fact*. If one part is true in fact, the other can be true only by analogy or exaggeration. Using figures of speech is perfectly fine as long as the listener/reader knows that they are not direct contradictions.

Factual contradictions are *always* errors of thinking. When we find a contradiction, we know with absolute certainty that we need to do more thinking, Many people would say that this is our unfortunate human weakness, proving that our thoughts are often wrong. Actually, it is a great strength.

We should be celebrating the fact that our natural method of thinking provides for a simple test of completeness. If two things cannot possibly be true in the given context, we know to examine the context more deeply to find the explanation.

Sometimes people try to disguise the fact that their statements contain errors, as in these two examples:

A. I do and I **don't**, and I **don't** want to talk about it.

B. It is and it **isn't**. Of course, we all know that. (Implying that it's **not** open to question).

In each of these examples, the person is making two statements. A contradictory statement and a refusal to explain. In example A, the refusal is an example of Emotion Overriding Facts. In example B, the refusal is an example of a major logical fallacy, the Fallacy of Numbers. We discussed both of these types of mistakes earlier in this chapter.

Sometimes people muddle the facts so that it is seems impossible to separate the opposites or get to the facts. This muddling always serves the purposes of anyone who wishes to confuse or take advantage of people.

OTHER EXAMPLES

We could add many more examples of negative statements to this list. People use negatives everywhere. People who stop you can be parents, teachers, enemies, or friends.

Sometimes, you use negativity to stop yourself. When something or someone stops you, you begin to feel powerless. Power is strength, muscle, control, or ability. When you feel powerless, you feel frustrated and out of control.

You saw that Janie felt frustrated and powerless when her father stopped her from running into the street. At two years old, Janie was easy for her parents to stop. And they started a good plan for teaching Janie what she needed to know to cross the street.

In this chapter you learned how to recognize the most common errors in thinking, including the most important, the claim of contradiction.

Whoever you are and however old you are, you're too old for your parents to stop you easily. They may never have had a good plan to teach you anything. They may have had the best of intentions, but not the knowledge or the dedication to put it into action.

Whatever your parents' powers or shortcomings, since you're reading this book, you have it in *your power now* to get what you need for yourself. Forget advantages. Forget disadvantages. You can take control. You can understand how you can create a positive, happy life for yourself.

Maybe your parents had a great plan, and you feel great about yourself and your life. Maybe they gave you this book to read, and you're reading it to confirm everything they taught you. That would be awesome!

Now that we have the information on negativity, in the next chapter, we can zoom ahead into the positive territory – the real-life practical approach to finding and doing Job 1, the Job you can do now!

Let's GO!

8. Staying Centered on Job 1

We are what we repeatedly do. Excellence, then, is not an act, but a habit.

— Aristotle

Job 1 is the engine of your success. Why? Job 1 is the *only* job you can do.

Since the beginning of this book, I've been telling you that Job 1 is the only job that you can do. And I stand by that, but that's not the whole story of Job 1. This chapter is going clarify your understanding of Job 1.

Now you're going to find out that there are actually two different types of jobs called Job 1:

A. Practical Life Jobs: Jobs you don't have to think about but you need or want to do.

B. Job Stack Jobs: Jobs you've thought about, set up, and are ready to do through your own plans or reading *Liftoff* and the training you're getting now.

99

You learned many practical life skills when you were a kid: feeding yourself, tying your shoelaces, etc. Now you do them automatically. When you eat, you think about the flavor of your food, not the skill you need to hold a fork or cut your meat. As an adult, you need to know how to clean up after yourself, wash any dishes, dry them, and put them away. As a teen, it's time to learn and make adult life your habit.

PRACTICAL LIFE JOBS

You will always have many more practical life jobs that you can do without too much thought than you have jobs (1, 2, or 3) in your Job Stack. You have a universe of jobs in the "Don't even think about" category. But you can't do them because the only job you can do is Job 1.

I hope you're beginning to realize that there's no use wasting any time thinking about jobs you cannot do because you don't know how to do them and you're not ready to think about how to do them.

What do you do if you don't have a Job 1 on your list? You do all the jobs of practical life that you can do today without much thinking. You put them on your list as "Today's Job 1." You do them all until none are left. You will get a good idea of how long these routine jobs take. You will also learn which jobs go together well and how many you can do on any particular day.

Here are the types of Job 1 jobs that you need to do automatically and routinely as a well-organized teen:

↗ Get dressed

↗ Make your bed

↗ Wash your clothes

↗ Hang up your clothes or fold them and put them in drawers

↗ Keep your room neat

↗ Empty your wastepaper basket

↗ Take out the garbage

↗ Cook meals

↗ Count your money, keep track of it, and spend it wisely

↗ Provide for money coming in

↗ Shop for food and clothes

↗ Many more....

You may not think any of these tasks is special. However, if you decide you're going to be the adult you want to be proud of, you need to do all of these things well, and routinely. You shouldn't need anyone to tell you, nag you, or promise to pay you to take care of your own life and surroundings. You will figure out a way to keep doing them as a routine of your practical, real, adult life.

Of course, when you're working in a business or selling something, you're providing for money coming in. Your customer or employer will pay you. However, there's a lot of variability in family allowances. In general, you should not expect or take money from your parents when you do routine chores around the house. They've provided for you since the day you were born.

Do your parents pay you to make your bed, clean your room, and clean up after yourself? These are the things that your parents did for you when you were a little kid. You should be doing them for yourself now.

Do your parents pay you to do the dishes, cook, or take care of younger children? Some parents can afford this, but realistically, others cannot.

Your parents want you to learn the value of money by earning it. They would like you to learn to save money and spend it wisely. The less money they have, the less they can afford to give you an allowance. When you're a young teen, you can't even work a regular job, so that makes the situation harder for you and for your parents.

You need to learn empowerment. You learn empowerment by taking responsibility for your own life. Empowerment requires more than just having money and knowing how to save and spend it wisely. Empowerment requires success, because it cannot happen without it. If you want people to treat you like an adult, act like an adult.

You're going to have to act like an adult when you're an adult. You don't have to give up on the kid in you, especially the kid who likes to have fun. You have to reject the kid in you that doesn't like to take responsibility. Take a look at the chain again:

Failure →*Experience*→*Progress*→*Success*→*Purpose*→ **Empowerment**

If you're an older teen and have a paying job, your parents may feel that they shouldn't have to pay you to do chores. If money is tight, they may need you to contribute to the household, since you're earning a paycheck.

Every family's financial situation is different. You want to find a solution that works for *all* of you.

One approach might be to get an allowance for common chores that help everyone, such as laundry, dishes, and ironing. Another approach is to offer to do things for your parents that, otherwise, they would pay someone else to do.

Cooking and serving a meal from start to finish, including cleaning up, might be a great way to earn an allowance. Try a Kids Cook campaign to assert your responsibility.

Instead of approaching the subject of money with the typical teen attitude, *I need more,* shock your parents by approaching the situation as an adult would do it and negotiate. Look around at your home. Look at them as if you were an adult yourself.

Are there chores, repairs, or improvements that no one is doing? Is something broken that you can fix? Do your parents take work home that you could help with? Are your parents stressed and overwhelmed?

What would they think if you offered to make breakfast on the weekends, including cooking it, serving it, and cleaning up? Wouldn't that be a treat for them and a nice accomplishment for you?

Is your family garage full of junk? You can offer to clean it out. Is any of the junk saleable? You could offer to run a garage sale and take 40% of the proceeds.

Do your parents have things they don't use but you could sell for them and earn a commission on Craig's List? Can you babysit, walk dogs, or shovel snow? Can you mow lawns, run errands, or wash cars in your neighborhood? Can you sew? Can you build stuff?

When you approach them with any new idea, be prepared to have them laugh at you! Don't let their laughter hurt you. They're not used to you behaving as an adult, and it will take them some time to realize that you're ready to take responsibility.

The key question is: what can you do for your parents or your family that they'll be eager to pay for and you'll be proud to do for them?

By the way, if your parents promised you money for reading this book, show them that you've already learned a valuable lesson. Tell your parents that you cannot accept the money and they need to read *Liftoff,* too.

Practical life often involves previously learned things that you need to do. Someday, you'll be an adult. You might have a car. Will you run it until it runs out of gas before you get to the gas station? Will you do regular maintenance to make sure it runs well and stays in good shape? What will you do when you have your own apartment or house? Will you make a routine to keep it nice, clean, and well-maintained?

Taking care of practical life as well as you can is the number one Job 1, no matter who you are or how old you are.

This type of Job 1 confirms things you know. It deals with practical life. It keeps the level you are already at as good as required for smooth adult life.

Sometimes, Job 1 is something you know you need to do, and you know how to do, but you don't want to do it. You've been procrastinating, delaying, and hoping Mom or someone will do that job for you or make it go away.

For that, there's only one answer:

C'mon, _____, put on your big kid pants and do Job 1.

Practical life jobs often contain a series of tasks. When you were little, you watched grownups do them. You may have helped with some of the tasks. As a teen, it is time for you to know how to do the job and all its tasks from start to finish. Cooking your own breakfast is a good example. Here is a sample Job 1 sequence that you as a teen should be able to do:

1. Get the ingredients, dishes, utensils, and pots you will use.

2. Cook your breakfast.

3. Eat breakfast.

4. Wash the dishes, utensils, pots when you're finished.

5. Dry the dishes etc.

6. Put the dishes etc. away.

Those six tasks are one job. Of course, if you have a dishwasher, you can just load the dishwasher. But for a one-person meal, you may not want waste all the water or stick around to put the dishes away. Sometimes it's easier and quicker just to wash everything you used, dry it and put it away. You're done, and nobody needs to remind you to put the dishes away later.

The whole job includes cleaning up after you've achieved your goal. If your job is to cook an egg, the whole job includes getting the egg, cooking it, eating it, and cleaning up after yourself.

Doing Job 1 should not leave a new job for you or anyone else to do. By making one part of your life better, you should not be leaving an undone job for another part of your life or for someone else.

When you do a practical life job, you want to observe the principle of *minimal disruption*: doing Job 1 should not leave things worse than when you started. It should not leave a new job for you to have to think about or for anyone else to do. In the case of eating your breakfast, the goal is to feed yourself, which you did in step 3, but the job includes leaving the kitchen neat and clean after you've achieved your goal.

Job 1 of practical life is the job you can do, know how to do, and don't have a good reason not to do. You may or may not want to do a job. By doing your own jobs, you demonstrate maturity. By doing your chores willingly and efficiently, you demonstrate maturity. By respecting your family, you earn respect in return.

Do you have to do everyone's job? No. You do your own jobs and the jobs that will make your life better. You clean your room and clothes. You feed yourself without waiting for someone to feed you. You study and do homework to make your grades better. If you need help with that, get it together and ask for help.

These practical life Job 1s may nag at you, but if you do them, you can cross them off your To Do List.

If you manage your practical life and Job Stack in this way, staying centered, you'll be continually growing in accomplishment and efficiency. Your accomplished jobs will start piling up, and your spirits will rise as your level of accomplishment rises. You'll have *Liftoff*.

JOB STACK JOBS

Job 1 is the center of your achievement. While you're doing your practical life jobs, you'll be thinking about your Job Stack Job 2 and Job 3.

Your subconscious will bring suggestions to your conscious mind about what pieces you could set up in Job 2 or what you could think about next in Job 3. These "suggestions" from your subconscious would occur like fleeting thoughts.

Your conscious mind would decide *yes* or *no*. If it is a good idea, your subconscious mind is helping to make your Job 2 and Job 3 easier for you to think about or to set up. Yay!

Your subconscious mind will be free from stress because you're doing all the jobs you can do in an orderly fashion. You'll begin to get ideas of how you can break off a piece of Job 2 so you can do it now. Wow! That would be a Job Stack Job 1. When you finish the next practical life job (completely), do your new Job Stack Job 1. You'll thank yourself right then, and later too!

Your three needs are:

↗ Live your everyday life as best you can with a minimum of negatives (stress).

↗ Learn and do new things to keep your life fresh and exciting.

↗ Enjoy your life. Have fun.

HOW TO BACKTRACK

If you decide that the jobs in your Job Stack, the jobs of your What-to-Do, are too hard or will take too long to do, there's a solution for that: backtrack.

Answer these questions:

1. Can you make the What-to-Do easier by making it smaller? If yes, do it. If no, keep going down this list.

2. Can you find a different, easier What-to-Do from the same positive statement? If yes, do it. If no, keep going.

3. Can you find a different negative statement that you can transform? If yes, do it and make a new What-to-Do. If no, keep going.

4. Can you make a new negative statement that you can transform? If yes, do it. Make a new positive statement. Make a new What-to-Do. If no, keep going.

5. Do you have some practical life jobs you need to do and can do? If yes, think about how long it will take you to do at least some of these practical life jobs today. Set aside

some time to do them. Make a list. Call them "Today's Practical Life Job 1 list."

6. Work through the jobs on your practical life Job 1. While you're doing your practical life Job 1s, you'll be letting your subconscious do the work of finding and suggesting which What-to-Do might be easiest for you.

7. Now that you've finished all your practical life Job 1s, go back to question 1 and see if you can answer anything as positive to release yourself. If no, keep going.

8. Make a new negative statement, "I don't understand the Job Stack." Make a positive statement specifically about what in the Job Stack you don't understand that you want to understand. Make your What-to-Do: I would like to find out the answer to this question, and write the question. If you have a question that you think I haven't covered in the book, please explain your question as fully as you can in terms of what you have done and where you're having difficulty. Share your story or ask a question at liftoff4teens.com.

CONFIDENCE

Confidence comes from accomplishment. Self-empowerment comes from continual accomplishment. You get to the next level by learning new things, breaking new ground, and making what you've learned in practical life into good habits.

You can be like a ball of energy. When you lift your spirits by your own accomplishments, you keep the excitement of life. You've seen cartoon characters who show competence and energy.

They whirl around a room and clean up all the mess in no time flat.

At the beginning of this chapter, I told you that there are actually two different types of jobs called Job 1. There are the jobs of practical life that you know how to do and hardly have to think about, which you need to do to live a smooth and stress-free adult life. Then there is the job that you thought about when you chose to turn the negatives that limit you into positives you can achieve. You've set up that job on your Job Stack. It's the job that you're ready to do to get yourself to the next level.

It should be obvious to you that must do your practical life jobs and the jobs that crush your negatives with positive action. You must do them both.

"It's not who you are underneath, it's what you do that defines you."

—Batman Begins (2005)

You do all your jobs that are Job 1 in turn. You make a habit of doing them all, and doing them well. It will be a good habit, and good habits get you to the next level.

9. Practical Thinking

Thinking is the human means of survival. This means that we use our minds to know the world because we have to figure out what to do to stay alive.

In Chapter 8, we learned more about Job 1 – the job we can do because we know how to do it and we're ready to do it. In this chapter, we'll concentrate on Job 2, the job we have thought about and are ready to set up.

Since big projects usually have many steps, we need to understand what to do step by step. We'll use Checklist #1 to clarify practical thinking.

The checklist is a learning tool. You use the paper tool until you know it automatically. You're familiar with knowing things automatically. If you needed to add 6 + 8, you wouldn't need to write it down. You learned that in first or second grade and it is part of you.

You can learn to use Checklist #1 in a similar way. You write it down until you don't need to write it down. Then write it down only when you need to check whether anything is missing.

WHY—PURPOSE

The first box on the checklist is your statement of purpose, your "why." Your entry should be the simple reason for the particular action you plan to take.

"Why" explains the purpose.

For example, you may be looking for your first paying job in a company. You might say that your reason for taking that job is to earn more money than you can earn babysitting, dog walking, or the other odd jobs we talked about in Chapter 8. But since there is usually more than one job available, you should know why you want to take that particular job.

It could be that it's the only job you can get without having prior experience. Since you can only get one first job in your life, this job would teach you about what jobs are like. Even if you don't like the job, you would get some job experience. That would be a deeper reason. Getting job experience is important.

Maybe you want a particular type of job. If you get that type of job, you'll learn a lot and you think you'd enjoy it. If your purpose were to get that type of job, you would have two deep reasons important to your mental health: learning on the job and enjoying the job.

When you think of your purpose, you might have only a superficial reason at first. You may have to answer more of the questions in the checklist before you can give a deep answer.

We use "purpose" to stand for the many words that answer the question "why?" Words like goal, motive, cause, reason, idea, or principle are a few more that answer the question "why?"

When you know your purpose, you can identify what you need to think about, prepare, and do. Purpose is not always in the future. Sometimes, your purpose might be to discover the cause of something that happened in the past.

THE LANGUAGE OF PRACTICAL THINKING

There are three additional terms we use for practical thinking: *context, thing,* and *characteristics.*

When we use the word *context*, it's our standard term for many related words. Other common words for context are situation, setting, background, framework, environment, perspective, and circumstances.

The word *thing,* is a very general word that can mean:

A. Physical entity or happening such as an object, item, device, or event

B. Any living being

C. Stories, myths, and dreams

D. Absences, negatives, or unknowns

E. Any noun, idea or concept

Characteristic is also a very general term that can mean feature, appearance, type, description, or attribute. For physical things, characteristic refers to classes of descriptions such as color, texture, sound quality, taste, or substance. Characteristic also describes specific observable or measurable qualities such as length or weight.

Symbols also have characteristics. Concepts are symbols in our minds that stand for things in the world outside our minds. The sounds of words and the shapes of the letters are characteristics of our concepts as we use them in our everyday life. The meaning of the concepts exists only in our minds. The sounds that we hear and the images we read as words are characteristics of the concepts that exist in our minds.

CONTEXT—WHAT, WHO, WHERE, WHEN

What, who, where, and when are questions that set the **context** of the situation. Putting things in context means understanding the what, who, where, and when about an entire situation. So the context includes everything in the situation except our purpose and the actions we will take.

Context sets the limits of the situation.

The context does not include the "why" or the "how." We've already talked about the "why," the purpose. We'll get to the "how" shortly.

WHAT—THE THING WE WANT TO AFFECT OR THE CAUSE WE WANT TO USE.

When you're thinking about something, that **Thing** is what you're thinking about in your context.

The Thing is what we're talking about in the context.
Characteristics of things give us information about things.

Some things are characteristics of other things. This can be very confusing to talk about, but we all learned to understand this implicitly when we learned to talk.

For example, "The ball is red" tells us that the thing (ball) has a general characteristic (color) that has the specific characteristic (red).

Why is this important? As we learn new things, we want to reuse principles we already know. When the context expands, we need different specific information in order to use the same principle in a different context. For example, you'd use your knowledge of balance to learn to ride a bike, skateboard, or hover board.

WHO, WHERE, WHEN—THE AGENT(S), PLACE AND TIME

Every context includes who, where and when, the person or people involved, the place and time. We think about who, where and when to get the complete picture. You saw this clearly when you used Checklist #1 to tackle your own jobs to get from Level I to Level II.

When we can reuse principles by recognizing the specific information, the characteristics of the things we have in the new context, we can get to the correct effect faster and with less effort. Thinking in principles is not only more efficient, it's easier and more successful than the hit-and-miss methods used by most people.

It also shows that context must be appropriate to the purpose in order to satisfy the purpose.

HOW—THE ACTION(S) STEP BY STEP

In thinking in principles, we separate the action from the context because the action is how we're going to change the context.

When you decide on your action steps, you're making your roadmap to positive achievement. Your steps will include actions you need to take before you can actually start doing the job. This type of actions might include permissions, training, or research. You might have people interested in doing the job with you. They might work for you.

For big goals, the action steps may be complex. Each step or set of related activities might become a separate job. This is especially true when you're doing something for the first time. You may want to take it slowly and pay attention to each action as it occurs. You don't want to miss anything important. Later, when you know exactly how each action flows, you can streamline.

The action defines the context before and after.

When you're working on the step of completing the job, you want to observe each action for a different reason. You want to know whether the job is on target to satisfy your purpose. If it isn't, you might have to do the step over, so that's important.

When you have a clear purpose, it drives your life. Every moment of joy, every moment of struggle, is your moment in the treasure that's your life. You live the life you're empowering yourself to love.

Humans advance as thinking advances. As an individual, you can advance as your thinking becomes clearer and more focused. As your thinking becomes clearer, the thinking process becomes easier. You waste less time and effort.

10. Empowerment and the Broken System

In *Liftoff*, you're learning the tools and skills you need to live and work in a free society. In a free society, individuals act on their knowledge and use their abilities to earn the values that make their own lives the best they can be.

However, our social system is actively working *against* empowerment. You need to understand that and prepare for it. You need to be armed with the knowledge that self-empowerment is good. You need to decide that you are worthy of self-empowerment.

When faced with a problem or challenge, the self-empowered individual thinks, *I can learn it. I can do it. I will do it!* This is the attitude of self-empowerment.

In the self-empowered society, people trade values cooperatively, each one with the purpose of making his own life better. By now, I think you agree that self-empowerment is good.

Unfortunately, our negative culture can block you from seeing value in others and block others from seeing your value for them.

When faced with a problem or challenge, our society teaches you helplessness: *you can't learn it. You can't do it. Don't even think about it.*

Does this sound familiar? Does this remind you of how you felt about your own negatives in Chapter 1? You see, the problem was never only you. The problem is that our progressive society is destroying empowerment.

Liftoff started with you because you needed to find the positive within yourself. When you recognize the positives in yourself, you are ready to see the positive value in others. You are also ready to understand why others may not be able to see value in you: they do not see positive values in themselves.

Liftoff is about growing your own empowerment. First comes understanding the idea of empowerment. Next comes practicing your skills and succeeding at small jobs.

Then comes the big step of allowing yourself to make mistakes, fix the mistakes and *learn from experience*. Your small successes will help you convince yourself that *you are worthy*.

That conviction will help you to find and succeed at your life purpose.

Self-empowerment is the key to the drive and energy of the productive person. To achieve your best possible life as an adult, you need to hold on to your commitment to the self-empowerment that is naturally within you. In Chapter 13, you will see how self-empowerment is naturally within you.

Whatever purpose you choose, whether your goals are modest or great, as long as self-empowerment is your driving force, your life will be a benefit to you and to everyone with whom you come in contact.

Right now, as a teen, you need to learn to work successfully with other people. Seek out positive people. Avoid negative people. Your success now will arm you against the negative people you will encounter later.

At the end of this chapter, your assignment to complete Level II is to work with other people who are also trying to find and grow their own empowerment (whether they know about this book or not).

The destroyer of empowerment is *entitlement*. In today's culture, entitlement means deserving of the *unearned* by right.

Entitlement originally meant *deserving by right.* Upstanding adults deserved respect; people struggling with an infirmity deserved pity; achievements deserved admiration; and people we liked deserved our friendship.

It was right for us to grant the respect, pity, admiration and friendship to people as they deserved it because each one was *entitled*.

However, there was also an ugly, more sinister use of entitlement. The pharaoh was entitled to decide who lived and who died. The chief of the tribe was entitled to your cows and your chickens. The lord of the manor was entitled to rape your daughter. The cleric was entitled to behead infidels. Clearly, those types of entitlements are wrong.

We first saw the use of force as *Might Makes Right*, one of the common mistakes in thinking, (Chapter 7):

> *"The bully in the schoolyard beats you up. The adult tyrant makes a system to take your property and put you in jail or kill you if you disagree."*

Now in our progressive culture, entitlement means *deserving of material wealth by right*.

Who are the entitled? The list of entitled is long: the poor, the down-trodden, the helpless, the homeless, the political elites, the universities, the friends of the political elites, students, old people, sick people, disadvantaged ethnic groups, disadvant-aged religions, and victims of discrimination.

Who are the targets of the entitled? The producers of the material wealth: productive individuals. The entitled demand that productive individuals become productive robots.

If you're productive and successful, some people will demand your *disempowerment*. The more successful you are, the more demanding they will be.

Disempowerment was the evil that horrified me in kindergarten when I saw happy, playful children turning into docile robots. Another name for a docile, robot-like human is *slave*. A slave is a person who must obey.

A slave cannot express an independent opinion, hold a private thought or own private property. A slave is a non-person. A slave cannot escape his situation without risking his life.

An angry slave with an ounce of humanity rebels against his slavery. A docile robot accepts its fate. It knows no better.

The productive person who gives up the products of his self-empowerment has less incentive to achieve. The people who become *entitled* to receive the unearned from the productive person have *no* incentive to achieve.

When the entitled person enslaves the productive one, both are losers. The productive person loses his property, the material values that he produced. The entitled person loses more; the entitled person loses his shot at self-empowerment. He enslaves himself to the institutions of entitlement. He loses not only his self-empowerment, but his self-direction, his self-discipline and most of all, his self-esteem.

It's a world-wide system. Some people see it as evil, and not merely broken. You will have to judge that for yourself.

Instead of encouraging productivity, the entitlement system encourages dependency. Instead of encouraging self-empowerment, it encourages powerlessness. The system has different names in different countries: communism, socialism, fascism, monarchy, theocracy and democracy.

It may surprise you that democracy is on this list, but pure democracy is majority rule with no provision to respect the rights of the individual. It was the democracy of Athens that sentenced Socrates to death for teaching the young men to question their elders. It was the democracy of the townspeople of Salem, Massachusetts, that burned people at the stake for being different, and assumed to be "witches."

The United States was not a pure democracy at its beginning. It was a federal republic with democratic elements. The government did have the obligation to protect individual rights. In a long political process taking over 100 years, that obligation has been set aside in favor of entitlements.

The simple fact is that without the obligation of the government to protect individual rights equally by an objective process of law, there is no difference in fundamental principle between communism, socialism, fascism, monarchy, theocracy or democracy.

People collect the money earned by the productive, by force of law. Others distribute the money to the entitled, also by force of law.

No one gets to keep his or her own money by right. Our society calls this the fair redistribution of income.

Bureaucrats run it. Politicians glory in it. The entitled depend on it.

In all of these types of governments, one simple rule describes what the government does:

> From each **productive** person according to his ability to **produce**.

> To each **entitled** person according to the **decision of the leaders**.

In a pure democracy, the majority rules, and the leaders carry out the wishes of the majority. The productive minority has no say or protection under the law.

The United States was the only country founded on a different idea. At its founding, the United States rejected the old system of confiscation and handouts. Instead, the Constitution recognized the principle that each person was the owner of his own life.

Each individual was self-empowered to live his life in pursuit of his personal goals and happiness. The power of the government was to be solely to stop the violation of rights. It would be wrong to force an individual to act against his self-interest. His self-interest was his to decide and pursue, as long as he didn't violate the rights of others.

Now, in fact, the Constitution was not perfect. There were many problems. The greatest error was that the Constitution enshrined chattel slavery. The Constitution promised to consider all men equal, *with the notable exceptions of all slaves and all women.*

In another section, the Constitution promised to protect the rights and property of its citizens, *with the notable exception of actions taken for the public welfare.*

The Constitution made exceptions to its principle that each person is the owner of his own life. That was its downfall. When a principle contains exceptions, it means that the "principle" is not really a principle.

The "principle" contains a contradiction. Does the Constitution protect the rights of *all* the people or only *some*? Which is it? The Founders may have thought *all*, but the language of the Constitution the Founders enacted entitled only *some.*

The contradiction is destroying the free society that the Founders tried to achieve.

In Chapter 11, we will discuss how to get clarity by thinking in principles. Thinking in principles is another important tool that will add strength to your empowerment. Before we go on to Level III, you need to consolidate the material you've learned in Level II by applying it to working with others.

People you encounter all have individual levels of self-direction and self-discipline. They may inspire you to do better, or you may inspire them. Your experience working with others will help you understand how their purpose, context and skills can mesh with yours to produce the best results.

When people have compatible goals, they can get excellent results. When people working together have strong self-direction and self-discipline as well, the results can be amazing.

COMPLETING LEVEL II

We're very close to completing Level II. Here's what I said you would learn in Level II:

↗ In *Level II*, you'll learn about the widespread negative beliefs in our culture. You'll learn to choose the positive. You'll understand when and how to work with friends or groups.

Let's have a quick review of the massive amount you've learned in Level II:

↗ In Chapters 6 and 7, you learned about many common thinking errors. As in Level I, the correct approach is to confirm positive beliefs by positive action.

↗ In Chapter 8, you learned that you need to know how do the practical life jobs that adults do to keep their lives running smoothly. You learned, in Aristotle's words that:

We are what we repeatedly do. Excellence, then, is not an act, but a habit.

↗ In Chapter 9, you learned about purpose, context and action. We connected these ideas to the six essential questions of Checklist #1. You learned that we separate the action from the context because action changes the context. To learn by experience, we need to control the changes.

↗ In Chapter 10, you learned about entitlement and its role in destroying empowerment.

For all the writing you did for Level I, I promised that Level II wouldn't require writing. However, I also said that in Level II, you might *want* to keep a list of who is doing what.

If you plan to be a motivator of people, such as a leader, teacher or boss, you should pay close attention to the individual purposes of people. To get to Level III, and know you belong there, you need to know how to work with other people.

Here's what I said you would do in Level III:

↗ In *Level III*, you'll learn that the capacity for empowerment is naturally within you. You'll gain self-empowerment from your positive experiences and choices.

In our preparation for Level III, let's begin with the questions from Checklist #1 to form the instructions for this assignment:

Why? Why is working with others part of a book on self-empowerment?

You need to learn how your self-empowerment can enhance your cooperative work. In your jobs and in your relationships, you will seek positive people. You want people to respect you as an individual. You want to respect them.

Doing activities with others will make respect and empowerment real for you. Adding people to the job flow takes effort, but when done well, the effort is worth it.

What? What should you do? Here are guidelines you should use to decide what *you will do.*

Your assignment is to complete five jobs you can do over five days. At least two of those jobs should include working with one or more other people.

You can continue with your Job Stack jobs, writing out only what suits you. If you use the Job Stack form (Worksheet #3), you can add your partner's activities to the steps for a complete picture of the jobs.

In Level II, you saw many more examples of types of jobs you might want to do. Whether you write extensive notes, or a simple To Do List is a matter of your time and temperament. For complex jobs, you may choose to write more.

Who? Will you do this alone? Who will work with you? In this assignment, you want to learn how to keep you own goals and make working with someone else a good experience.

There will be jobs or steps that you continue to do alone. Some steps *require* people to work together, like moving heavy furniture. Other steps complement each other, like washing dishes and drying them.

You can relate the steps in the Job Stack for this assignment to a common purpose. You might have a Family Projects Job Stack, a Library Study Group Job Stack, or a Class Trip Job Stack. You could work with people and not tell them about the Job Stack. In that case, you would try to understand their motivation and goals as a way to understand how to work with them better.

You can find opportunities to work with a partner or a group of people. Families, friends, school, or clubs are opportunities for interaction.

Where? When? These questions will contain your answers based on the place and time of the jobs.

For example, if you're on a team, you can practice with someone at a field to improve your skills. If you're in a play as cast or crew, you have many opportunities for cooperation.

In any group, team, family or job, you want people in the group to recognize your contribution. You make that happen by recognizing their contribution.

How? Before:

If you're working for someone else on a job, think of what you want to get out of the job. You may be able to see a way to take action to get more out of the job, or put more into it.

In each case of working with others or in a group, your efforts should be of value to the group effort. Getting permission or confirmation is a step in doing the job. If you need confirmation, don't skip asking for it.

How? During:

You've worked with other people many times. Now when working with others, you want to match your own *self-discipline* and *self-direction* with theirs for the best result. This means that each of you has an understanding of the purpose, and is willing to share both the drudgery and the joys of working together.

People who work together must respect each other to get good results. Even if the person or people in your group don't know about *Liftoff*, you should still show them the respect of understanding their purpose, context and goals.

As a teen in a family, if the members of your family respect you as a person, they will be teaching you to respect them. Unfortunately, respect doesn't happen in every household. Many will tell you that you must do things for people and then people will respect you.

This is incorrect. You must *thank* people who do things for you. You must thank them for the specific things they do.

Always be sure to actually say *thank you.* Then you can ask them if you may do a specific thing for them or with them to help them. They won't always say yes to what you propose, *but they will respect you for asking*.

When people start to respect you, they will treat you with respect. You will get *thanks* from them. Accept *thanks* graciously. You will feel good about respecting people and good when they respect you, too.

Of course, you could skip doing the assignment and continue to work on your jobs alone. However, you *know* that you should challenge yourself to get out of your comfort zone. If you're used to working alone, make the effort to find someone to work with you on something. Rising to the challenge will increase your social skills.

Once again, it's up to you.

C'mon, _____, put on your big kid pants and deal with 5 jobs over 5 days, at least 2 jobs or steps involving other people. You can do it!

Do your jobs. Work with family, friends, schoolmates. Pace yourself. Celebrate your successes. Learn from your experience.

In the next chapter you'll add to your thinking expertise by thinking in principle. It's easier than you think. When you think in principles, your thinking becomes super-efficient.

Thinking in principle might seem like a personal exercise. However, it has wide applications in the world. This is particularly true if you want fix the broken system.

Level III

↗ In *Level III*, you'll learn that the capacity for empowerment is naturally within you. You'll gain self-empowerment from your positive experiences and choices.

Welcome to Level III. You've come a long way and learned a tremendous amount. You should be rightly proud.

These final chapters will help you put all the material you've learned on a rock-solid foundation.

11. How to Think in Principles

Principles are statements or rules that guide you. Principles identify basic facts about the world.

Often, you're using a principle and you don't even know it. For example, when you were about 5 months old, you learned to sit up. Between 6 and 9 months, you learned to crawl and stand. You took your first wobbly step, and then your second one. You fell. You got up. You were determined. You walked! A month or two later, you ran!

You didn't know that balance is a principle, but you used it. You *felt happy* you were doing something right. You mastered balance with your whole body. When you ran, you felt like you owned the universe. Each level of balance led to a harder level, and when you ran, you celebrated. You used the principle of balance to achieve your goals of standing, walking, and running. You were using the principle of balance to guide each advance you made.

There's another sense of the word *balance* that applies here. As a toddler, when you learned to walk and run, you were learning physical balance. Now, when you learn the Job Stack, you are learning about *mental* balance.

If you try to do too many jobs, especially out of order, your life can become unbalanced, and you crash. The principle of mental balance answers the question of how many jobs you should do. The Job Stack helps you set good stopping points for the jobs you can't do now. You want to challenge yourself without overwhelming yourself.

We've already talked about another principle in this book. The principle of readiness answers the question what job do you do first. The answer is always Job 1. The reason is that you can only do Job 1. Job 1 is the job you can do now. Putting your jobs in order based on readiness and basing readiness on facts is using the principle of readiness to guide you on what you do.

When you know the outcome of an action in advance, you know whether you'll succeed. Thinking in principles gives you a reasonable expectation of good results, when you act accordingly.

A fundamental principle explains the action in a wide context.

If the principle you've found works, it will always work when you use it appropriately. Your purpose must be appropriate for the principle. You must pay attention to the context, the setup, and the steps you need to achieve your purpose.

If you don't pay attention to the context and the steps, your results will be unpredictable.

No principle can explain action beyond its context.

You've probably heard the saying, "The exception proves the rule." No, the exception does not prove the rule. The exception proves you're not following the rules of the principle. The exception proves the rules you're following are wrong for the purpose the principle can achieve.

Your knowledge can continually advance if you think in principles. You identify a purpose that serves your life. You perform actions that implement that purpose. You continually tweak and refine the context, the preparation, and the actions you take to achieve your purpose.

To know what to do, you need to get clarity. You want to have a clear idea of the facts that relate to your purpose, context and action. When you concentrate on the facts, you can discover the information you need to have reasonable certainty of outcome.

When we think in principles, we're on a quest to discover what causes are relevant to the effect we want to achieve. In Chapter 6, we talked about the principle of flight. Progress began only when people started asking questions that could have positive answers.

We can use Checklist #1 to demonstrate how you can think of the purpose, context and actions that pertain to the principles of flight and the birth of the aviation industry:

↗ **Purpose (Why):** To find out the causes of flight of birds and adapt those findings to human flight. To answer the questions: Could man achieve flight by bicycle power and stationary wings? What size wing would be necessary to raise a man into the air?

↗ **Context (What, Who, Where, and When)**: To observe the flight of birds in nature. To create an invention for human flight. To find a place and method suitable for testing human flight. To keep aware of all new developments and knowledge as they happen.

↗ **Actions (How)**: To identify the principles of flight that explain how birds fly.

- **Initial action**: To study aspects of bird flight such as wing flapping, gliding, soaring, circling, and slowing down to land.

- **Goal actions**: To invent and test human flight capability. To fly.

Bicycle power turned out to be inadequate. Instead, the Wrights used a specially-designed gasoline engine with a lightweight aluminum crankcase. The engine produced 12 horsepower. This proved to be adequate power per unit of weight to be successful.

To discover the principles of flight, people studied the characteristics of bird flight and bird anatomy in great detail. They did not know the principles of flight beforehand, they had to discover them. They observed and learned from particular birds and types of birds.

We call the process of observing things in the world and drawing a general conclusion *induction*. The general conclusion, the *hypothesis*, may be true or false.

The truth of the hypothesis is "proved" in action. If the hypothesis is correct, then people can create a specific new instance which demonstrates that the hypothesis is correct. The first sustained flight demonstrated that people were on the right track.

Flight is the effect people wanted to understand. To understand flight (the effect) people studied the characteristics of birds (flying creatures). They also studied the characteristic actions of wind and air. They called the study of the action of air *aerodynamics*. They adapted that knowledge for human requirements.

The answers to the question of flight came from this discovery, mentioned earlier:

> "Two key effects form the basis of all flight. The movement of the air over the wings creates the lifting force. The speed of the bird (or plane) pushes it through the air horizontally."

The Wright brothers demonstrated the principle of flight by making the world's first viable flying machine and then flying it. After years of thinking and trying different ideas, they succeeded in 1903. Flying the world's first airplane was the Wright brothers' Job 1. Their achievement changed the world.

In this example, the Thing (flight) depends on two characteristic actions (lift and speed) of specific things (birds) capable of flight.

As long as people talked in generalities, no progress was possible. Why do birds fly? Because they do. Why don't men fly? Because they're not birds.

The characteristics of things unlocked the principles. How do birds fly? The effect of air moving over the bird's wing lifts the bird higher. The effect of the bird's speed through the air is to keep it aloft.

In summary, principles are predictable because they tell us the effects of the characteristic of things. In the same or similar context, the same causes (actions), will result in the same or similar effect.

What are the actual causes of the effect? You could say simply that birds act according to their nature, which is to fly. However, that answer does not provide information to anyone wanting to understand what *in principle* causes any particular effect.

Some people take this short-cut and say that the cause of any effect is the *nature* of the thing acting or being acted upon. This formulation is still inadequate. To be clear, the nature of the thing is the totality of characteristics of the whole and of each part. To gain clarity, you must name the particular characteristic(s) responsible for any particular effect. This is the fundamental requirement of thinking in principle.

The answer, *in principle,* is that the effect on a particular thing is always a consequence of one or more characteristics of that thing and the characteristics of any other thing(s) that may be acting upon it. Author Betsy Speicher says it this way: *"The cause[s] of an effect are the characteristics of Things."*[5]

Here is a simple example of cause and effect relating to the characteristics of things:

> The outside surface of a pitcher of lemonade becomes wet on a hot day. The *coldness of the pitcher cools the surface of*

the pitcher. The cold surface of the pitcher causes the *moisture in the air* to *condense.*

The coldness of the lemonade and the moisture of the air cause the condensation on the pitcher.

Now you're getting ready to think in principles yourself. Use Checklist #1 to think about the details and set up your Job 2 steps. The checklist is only a guide to your thinking. It will not replace thinking. When in doubt, write things down.

Purpose:

Decide on your purpose. If your purpose is multi-level, know all of your purposes. The surface purpose is your practical purpose.

Every step in a job has a specific purpose. Deep purposes can be mental and physical. You need to know when you finish a step whether you accomplished your specific purpose completely, partially or not at all.

Context:

When you set the context, you are defining the situation that will satisfy your purpose with answers to the key questions: what, who, where and when. Answer all the questions about the characteristics of the things in your context that may be important to your purpose.

Actions:

Set up the actions you will do. Identify parts of the job dependent on earlier actions. Set the sequence of steps. Use references if you need them.

Refine the purpose, context and actions in terms of relevant characteristics of things. Eliminate dead ends. Disregard or limit unlimited negatives.

When you are ready, each step of the Job 2 will become Job 1 in its turn.

If you didn't fully accomplish your purpose in any particular step, turn the negative outcome to a positive statement and a positive what-to-do, and try again with a different characteristic or thing. Transform the failure into a learning experience.

For each step in a learning process, the main questions are: What do I know? What do I need to learn? How do I learn it? What should I do next? What characteristic of what thing is or has the answer? What should I change?

If a source book, person, or document tells you that thinking in principles is old-fashioned, impossible, or silly, look at the list of fallacies and negatives in Chapters 6 and 7 to see how that opinion is wrong. Get the strength to stick to your guns. You might not have the principle yet, but if you give up, you'll never have it.

Practice on easy jobs or practical life jobs first because they're easier and surer. Practice the principles of efficiency, readiness, and minimal disruption to make your practical life more organized and joyful.

Enjoy the process as well as the outcome.

Our work is almost finished. Don't worry if this seems overwhelming. Think of your first day of kindergarten, high school or college: overwhelming! The next two chapters are going to give you the final two pieces of the puzzle.

Perhaps you'll have an *"aha" moment* as I did when I realized why the Job Stack works. Then it will only be a matter of doing Job 1, one job at a time.

Of course, sometimes, you'll want to skip making a checklist. You could bog down if you made a checklist for every job you do. That's exactly why you want to concentrate on applying the three easy steps to practical life. When you're comfortable in the method, it will be automatic. When you make the Job Stack your habit, it will serve you for the rest of your life.

12. Reality and Contradiction

When I was 16, I had a school assignment that I didn't know how to tackle. I asked my father what he thought was the most important problem facing mankind today. His answer astonished me:

> **"The most important problem facing mankind today is that they cannot face it."**

I was shocked. I didn't know what the problem was, and he never told me. But I thought that deep down he must be right.

I decided that not facing the problem *was the problem.*

At 16, I didn't know the fundamental reason why people cannot face the problem. I didn't know that reality itself was the issue. I do know that now, and that's what this chapter is about.

Even our language is misleading when it comes to reality. I just wrote that *reality itself was the issue.* But of course, this is wrong. Reality is what it is. It can never be the issue.

In Chapter 1, you learned that your negatives limit you. By stating positives, you proved to yourself that you can break out. In Chapter 7, we explored one of the problems of negativity, apparent contradictions. You learned it is important to understand the claim of contradiction for two reasons:

↗ Claims of contradictions contain hidden negatives that limit you.

↗ Contradictions are always impossible *in fact.*

You saw that when we clarify apparent contradictions, we can resolve them.

In this chapter, we're talking about *Reality and Contradiction.* Clearly, reality is what it is. If we know that contradictions are impossible *in fact*, why are contradictions still a problem?

Contradictions are a problem because people use the word *reality* in two ways that seem to contradict each other. Contradictions cause confusion.

↗ Reality can mean the physical world – everything in the world except our minds.

↗ Reality can mean everything that exists, including our minds.

Which one of these two statements is right? In fact, there is only one reality, the reality that includes everything, including our minds.

To make this clear from another viewpoint, we can ask and answer two simple questions:

↗ Can contradictions exist in the physical world, the world excluding our minds? **No.**

↗ Can contradictions exist when we mean everything that exists, including our minds? **Yes.**

Thus if contradictions cannot exist in the physical world excluding our minds, but can exist when we mean everything in reality, then *it's only our minds that can contain contradictions.*

Therefore, the following statement is true:

Contradictions are errors of thinking...

However, that's still not the whole truth. For the whole truth, we need to know *why* we think of reality in these two different ways. Is there a good reason?

The answer is *yes.* There is an excellent reason! We *must* think this way.

Reality is what it is at any given moment. But we think of reality as what is, what was, and what we would change it to be. The context is the state of things at *a given time.* The actions we are thinking about may change the context *over time.*

So time as a concept appears twice in Checklist #1. Time appears in the context section — in the form of the question word, *when*. It appears again in the action section when we define *how* things will change in terms of *before* and *after.*

We need to think about what happens for every step of a complex job: before, during and after. Changes exist in sequence, so the context changes over time as we initiate and apply our actions.

When we think of time and the relationship of things over time, we are thinking through a change in the context. The question word "when" opens our minds to the past, present and future. Physical reality, the reality of all animals except humans, is simply what is now.

Animals can remember behavior patterns at certain times. Your dog might wake you up or want you to put food out at a certain time. But from the animal's point of view, the animal remembers the behavior and wants to execute it now.

We need to recall these points about practical thinking:

↗ Context sets the limit of the situation.

↗ The action defines the context before and after.

When we're trying to figure out what to do or what to think about something, time is always a factor in the context of our thinking, because change always takes place over time — even if the change is instantaneous, there is always a before and after. As we saw in Chapter 7, the question of *when* is in Checklist #1: Clear Thinking. Here's the full story about contradictions:

Contradictions are errors in thinking or changes in context.

For example, in physical reality, if something exists now as a fact, what we want to change it to doesn't exist now in the same place or the same way.

For example, we can imagine that **right now** a ball is in the pitcher's hand. Soon he will throw it and the batter will swing. The pitcher wants the batter to miss the ball.

The batter wants to hit the ball. The fielders get ready to catch the ball. The catcher gets ready to catch the ball if the batter misses it.

If the batter is successful, the ball will fly off the bat into the field. If the batter is very successful, he might hit a home run. If the batter misses the ball, the ball will wind up in the catcher's mitt.

Everyone playing the game has a different point of view of what they want to happen and what they should do. But there is only one ball, and it is in only one place at any one time.

The ball in one place is factual, but millions of people enjoy thinking of all the places the ball can go while playing or watching the game.

The context of the game changes over time. It starts out with two teams of different people with different strengths, abilities, strategies and concentration. It ends up with one team being the winner and the other the loser.

We could be perverse and say that the ball does not move. It started in the stadium and at the end, it is still in the stadium. That would show only that talking in generalities is simplistic and unhelpful, as are all apparent contradictions.

When we accept the idea that reality is contradictory by its nature, that's the true error. It may feel like there's no way out, but the way out of a contradiction is always clear thinking.

When we find an apparent contradiction, we know, beyond a doubt, we have an error or a change. We use apparent contradictions between physical reality and our minds to find our errors and our changes. There's no other way.

Whether we have misjudged the context a little or a lot is not the issue. Something is in error, something has changed, or will change. We have to figure out the error.

The issue is that we humans often wish that reality would be something else. In other words, we wish passionately for contradictions. We frequently cling to contradictions, hoping that somehow they'll be true for us, even though we know we're just fooling ourselves.

When we're disappointed, we habitually blame reality for not living up to our expectations.

What kinds of contradictions? All kinds. We want to stay up until all hours of the night, and not be tired in the morning. We want to have the freedom from responsibility of our childhood past. We want the freedom to do what we please in our future adulthood.

Our need to buy cool stuff is often beyond our ability to earn the money to pay for it. We want to eat what we like without exercising and not have to worry about unhealthy weight gain. In other words, we often don't want to examine our priorities, our logic, our whims, or our hopes.

We want reality to bend to our preferences. Not all of us have all of these problems of course, but most of us have some.

In summary, the problem is that we want the benefits of conflicting alternatives. We don't want any of the downsides. And we want to avoid the responsibility of making a choice if we are wrong. We can't have it both ways.

Can conflicting alternatives exist in the physical world outside our imaginations? Not literally. We saw this in Chapter 7 when we explored the "Claim of Contradiction."

When we are talking about our desires, the same principle applies. We must think of the consequences before acting on our whims, needs, wishes, and desires. We must pay attention to facts. If we try to disconnect ourselves from reality, we create contradictions in our minds. When we try to contradict reality, we lose, and we may make someone else lose.

Contradictions cannot exist outside of the human mind. Contradictions have never existed outside of the human mind, and they never will. As we saw in Chapter 7, people frequently make claims of contradictions, but the claims are quickly resolved with specific factual information.

More than that, my answer is not to reject your mind because it's capable of holding contradictions. My answer is to fix your thinking! This fact is worth repeating:

Contradictions are errors in thinking or changes in context.

A change in context is also an error in thinking if we refuse to recognize the change.

The crisis the world is facing today is the same it has faced throughout history. The crisis is the refusal to understand that reality is *everything* that is. It's only within the human mind that contradictions can exist.

We have all heard the expression, *you learn from your mistakes.* Contradictions are your mistakes. You think something is true, then you find out it's not. You made a mistake. Do you learn from it, or do you hang onto your false idea?

REALITY IS POSITIVE

The simplest form of positive is *it is.* The contradiction would be *it is not.* Which is true? One or the other is true, but it is a test of reality to find out which one. We hold them both in our minds, do the test, and see which is correct. Absences and negatives are placeholders we use as tools to think about things that are missing, or unknown.

The positive starts with what reality *is*, what the whole of reality *is*, what everything real *is*. And the first thing you can say about everything that's real is that *it is real.* Things that are not real *are not real.* Now that sounds like a silly way to say things, but think about it. Maybe read this paragraph again.

Reality is. It exists.

THE REALITY OF CAUSE AND EFFECT

If you doubt that reality is real, try dropping a brick on your toe. You can see if the falling brick causes you pain when it hits your toe. If you believe that reality might be real, you can simply imagine dropping a brick on your toe. That way, you can avoid the actual pain you would receive from an actual brick dropped on your actual toe.

Someone may tell you that she thinks reality is a matter of opinion. You can tell her to try dropping a brick on her toe.

Usually, people will quickly back down from saying that physical reality is not real. They will say that they meant your ideas and your emotions make your reality for you. They will tell you that since everyone has different ideas and emotions, it means that everyone's reality is different. They will tell you that there are no absolutes. Some people will tell you that what is true for them is not true for others.

Now if you're willing to say, tentatively, that you believe reality is real, at least physical reality is real, we're making progress, because the basic principle of reality is simple.

Reality exists absolutely, whether any of us believe it or not.

Saying that each person's ideas and emotions make their reality for them is a misunderstanding of the function of thinking. This is just a form of sloppy thinking. In other words, it's just a cover-up for not thinking at all.

HOW WE KNOW REALITY

Our senses are the basic way that we know reality. When our senses observe any part of reality, what the senses detect is necessarily positive. If there were nothing to detect, the senses would not detect it. The physical cause of every effect must have a substance and shape.

With our five senses, we detect all kinds of things. We see things, hear things, smell things, taste things, and feel things. Our sense of feeling gives us direct information about the thing: smooth, rough, hard, soft, cold, hot, dry, or wet. When we try to lift something, we find out whether it's heavy or light.

We feel things in the world outside our bodies and we feel things inside our bodies as well. We can feel sore throats, aches, pains, and wounds. We can feel full when we eat enough and nauseous when we eat too much. We can feel a special tingle of excitement when a person we like looks as if he or she might like us, too. Each of these sensations is due to real physical processes in our bodies, which we detect.

We can be more exact about the senses. Senses detect physical changes in the parts of our bodies. To put this in one word, our senses detect "sensations," the effects of things on our bodies. The sensation is the fleeting change.

As babies, we automatically translate sensations into perceptions. Then we make the perception process automatic. Perception is the process of recognizing groups of sensations. We cannot doubt perception, since if we see, hear, smell, or taste something, there must be a positive trigger for that perception to occur.

We can be right about the cause of the perception. We can be wrong about it. We can ignore it. Those are the only choices we have. No other choices are possible. Since sensations are fleeting, we can doubt whether we really felt the change or imagined it, but clearly that doubt is in the quickness of our understanding, not in the sensation.

The person who wants to know reality has multiple chances to act accordingly.

THE REALITY OF PHYSICAL THINGS

Every part of reality is real. What do I mean "real"? Since we said that reality is real, then every part of reality is real. Every part is *what it is*.

In terms of physical things, all physical things take up space and have shape, without exception. Even if the shape is irregular, amorphous or gaseous, a mass in physical reality always has a perimeter. The perimeter of a mass is its shape.

We call a physical thing that takes up space a thing in itself.

Basic concepts like reality are easy to demonstrate; you just point and say, "There." The concepts are difficult to talk about because pointing is so easy. The next example will address this difficulty by showing how three different creatures observe and react to reality. The three creatures are a spider, a dog, and you.

We can use the example of a red ball. "The ball is the color red" tells us that the thing (ball) has a general characteristic (color) that has the specific characteristic (red).

If the red ball is in the path of a spider, the spider goes around or over the ball. It might also stop or go back. The spider cannot perceive the ball as a ball, but it adjusts its movement because it cannot go through the ball. So the fact that the ball exists and is in the way of the spider is real.

The ball is a physical thing in itself. The spider is a living creature. It is also a physical thing in itself. The spider walks

155

around the ball without knowing anything about the ball except that it is there. The spider doesn't have words for ball or walking. The spider doesn't have words at all.

Now a dog comes along. A dog has a bigger brain than a spider. It sees the same physical thing, the ball. The dog picks up the ball in its mouth. Then it drops it. The dog can associate some things in themselves with other things. The dog can tell the difference between things. The dog remembers everything perceptually, what it can see, hear, smell, taste, touch, and do. Dogs can see and remember objects. Dogs can hear sounds, smell odors, and remember them.

The dog, like the spider has no words. But if the dog had words, it would have eight answers to the six checklist questions:

Who	This
What	This
When	Now
Where	Here / There
Why	Good / Bad
How	Do

In addition, the dog associates a sound with itself, its name. A puppy will recognize its name after a few training sessions. A dog will associate some sounds with actions and some sounds with things. The dog does a lot with a little. It will remember the differences between things by the characteristics of the things it has the capacity to remember. The rest of the dog's apparent smartness depends on its experience and training at perceiving things in its life.

Now you come along. You have words. You see the same ball that the spider walked around. It's the same ball that the dog picked up and dropped. The physical thing in reality is what it is.

You have a word for the physical thing, *ball.* You have a word for the general characteristic that we mentioned, *color.* You have a word for the specific characteristic that we mentioned, *red.*

Things that are characteristics of physical things are not less "real" than physical things; they are real in a different way. The red is a specific characteristic of the ball and the ball is a thing in itself.

The words are not characteristics of the ball at all. They're characteristics of your conception of the ball. Your observation of the ball did not change the ball. It changed your mind. You encountered a fact of reality, identified it, and stored the information. Therefore, your concepts are characteristics of your thought process, which is a characteristic of your mind.

We said that the words are characteristics of your conception of the ball. The words, like all your words, are in you. The concepts you use, the ideas and dreams you have, are characteristics of you.

Here's the chain of physical reality and characteristics of you:

↗ Your body is a physical thing that exists in the world.

↗ Your brain is a physical thing that exists in your body.

↗ Your mind is a characteristic of your brain.

↗ Thinking is a characteristic action of your mind.

157

↗ Your words: *ball, color,* and *red,* are characteristics of your thinking.

THE REALITY OF SYMBOLS

If everything that's real *is real,* then what is the reality of words? If the thing is "only" a word, an idea, an absence, or a placeholder for an unknown, it is real *as a symbol.*

> *A symbol is something that represents something else…especially a material object that's invisible.*[6]

The symbol represents its *meaning.* Thus, the principle of words as symbols applies equally to words representing positive things, properties of things, relationships between things, as well as negatives, absences, placeholders.

This is true even if a single mind is the only place a certain symbol exists and the thinker of it has no inkling of how the mind connects to the physical brain.

> *"The brain is one of the most complex and magnificent organs in the human body. Our brain gives us awareness of ourselves and of our environment, processing a constant stream of sensory data. It controls our muscle movements, the secretions of our glands, and even our breathing and internal temperature. Every creative thought, feeling, and plan is developed by our brain. The brain's neurons record the memory of every event in our lives."* [7]

In fact, all words are symbols, no exception. Some words stand for real things we can observe in the world: *trees, birds, people,* or *sky.* Some words stand for relationships, position, or time that we can also observe in the world: *together, below,* or *now.* Some words stand for absences or stops; they are placeholders for the absence. *Nothing, zero, negative, no, not,* and *none* are symbols satisfying the human need for placeholders to stand for things that are absent, missing, or unknown.

Symbols are real *as symbols* because they exist as characteristics of our thoughts. We learn these symbols when we learn language, and we store them in our heads with their meanings.

Since we are real in reality, our heads are real in reality. Somewhere in our heads, the information is stored and we can retrieve it whenever we want it. We don't know how we do it, but we get it done.

Do scientists have any concrete idea of how the brain enables the mind to think, write, read, and understand? The short answer is no. The longer answer is, they're working on it. The longest answer is that scientists are still groping in the dark. No one has explained how the characteristics of the physical brain give rise to the mind. Not yet.

Objects can exist in the world before humans think of them as symbols. The moon, once a great unknown in the sky, has symbolized order and mystery since ancient times.

It's important to understand that even if the object exists prior to it becoming a symbol in someone's mind, only a human can make it a symbol because symbols are characteristics of human thinking.

Humans create all symbols. Only humans create symbols. Many people can think of the same symbol in the same way. That is also a characteristic of human thinking. The symbol is real, as a symbol.

A physical object is a fact. It's neither true nor false. It simply is. A concept is an idea, a symbol. Concepts, like all ideas and symbols exist only in our minds, as symbols.

When the concepts in our minds agree with the facts, the concepts are true. When they don't agree, the concepts false or imaginary. Our advantage in using concepts instead of perceptual and associative memory is that concepts allow us to understand and store a vast number of facts and their relationships.

When our ideas match reality, to the extent of the purpose for which we intend to use them, they're true. When our ideas don't match reality, to the extent of the purpose for which we intend to use them, they're inadequate or false.

If we revise our ideas until we find the match, we find truth. If we don't, we're maintaining a contradiction. We're holding as true in our mind something we know to be false.

When we confuse objects with the symbols they represent, we create a contradiction in the reality of our mind. We're saying the object is the symbol at the same time that the symbol is the symbol.

Now we saw that the physical object had physical characteristics that were of the object. We saw that the symbol had characteristics of thought that were of the mind. The meaning of the symbol is always in the mind. The meaning is never a characteristic of the physical object.

Now you have the tools to understand the most important problem that mankind cannot face, and has never been able to face. We saw that at both the physical and symbolic level, contradictions are errors in thinking.

Humans perpetuate contradictions by not correcting their errors of thinking.

Contradictions are widespread and the most dangerous form of negatives. Many adults are content to "get by" with uncorrected errors in thinking.

They do and they don't. They will and they won't. It is and it isn't.

If you're afraid of losing yourself as you hurtle toward adulthood, it is that vision of the ambivalent soul, sometimes here, sometime there, that you want to avoid.

In my view, contradictions piling up are the source of many mid-life crises. In our next chapter, you're going to blast past this hazard by learning how to achieve and maintain lifelong, genuine harmony.

We are building a chain of three basics: thinking in principles, reality, and life. Next, I'm going to talk about life in a way that I'm sure will be new to you. You may wonder what "life" has to do with thinking and your success, but if you follow this chain of thought, you'll soon see that the cost of perpetuating contradictions is human anguish.

13. Mission Control

In this chapter, you'll learn that the source of all your power is your conscious and subconscious mind working together in harmony to survive. In the final chapter, you'll learn what to do and how to do it to achieve that harmony.

First, you need to understand why powerlessness is unnatural. The feeling of powerlessness comes from fighting against yourself.

Why is powerlessness against nature? To answer this question, here's the shortest course in biology, ever.

SHORTEST COURSE IN BIOLOGY

Life is conditional. To stay alive, every living organism must act to maintain the shape and substance of the body it is alive in, *without exception*.

All life builds on the processes of the simplest form of life, the single cell, *without exception*.

A cell membrane surrounds every cell. The cell membrane maintains the shape and substance of each cell.

A membrane is a selective barrier; it allows some things to pass through but stops others.[8]

The cell membrane keeps stuff inside the cell that belongs inside and keeps stuff outside the cell that doesn't belong inside, *without exception*.

Many single-celled organisms respond to the world around them, even though they have no brains, muscles, or specialized cells.

A living organism responds to stimuli to the extent that *the organism has the capacity to respond.* Its capacity to respond to stimuli is life-optimizing.

Powerlessness is unnatural because each life form, by its nature, has the power to stay alive.

Humans are living creatures. They're not above, beyond, or outside biology.

THE THREE ASPECTS OF THE MIND

What does it mean to fight against yourself? Your mind has three aspects, which have different capabilities and functions. The three aspects are: 1) conscious mind, 2) subconscious mind, and 3) emotions.

Used properly, your mind is a unified whole that you use to keep in harmony with the world. Used improperly, the three aspects fight each other and make your life a hell.

There are three common pronouns, "me, myself and I," that correspond to the three aspects of mind: emotions, subconscious and conscious mind. You can use these common pronouns to remind you of the proper role for each aspect of your mind.

Your conscious mind is your controller, director, and thinker. It is your "I." Your conscious mind says, "I command."

Your subconscious mind is your slave, robot, and follower of orders. Your subconscious mind is the deepest you. Your subconscious mind says, "The answer is somewhere within myself."

Your emotions tell you instantly how you feel about something. Is something good for me or bad for me? When emotions are strong, they're a call for action.

Your emotions want you to protect your mind and body from harm, and celebrate your happiness with feelings of joy. Your emotions correspond to "me."

Your emotions don't think; they don't follow orders. They don't answer why. Many times, it may seem that your emotions are a law unto themselves, and, in a way, they are.

EMOTIONS AND THE CALL FOR ACTION

Emotions and wishes are feelings. They include happiness, fear, sadness, anticipation, excitement, comfort, or many others. Emotions can trigger physical effects in your body.

These triggers can change your heart rate up or down. Fear can cause the hairs to rise on the back of your neck. Feelings of calm can cause your breathing to slow down and blood pressure to drop.

Emotions can arise from your memories of similar past experiences. You often remember your feelings well. Sometimes, the facts of your current situation may not apply to the emotions you're feeling. Many times, you don't remember the actual facts well.

In Chapter 7, you saw that it is a mistake to let your emotions override facts. Sometimes, emotions can be muddled or wrong. And here's the point: your subconscious mind is the keeper of your memories.

Your emotions don't care about your memories. When they want to save you, they want to save you NOW! When they want you to be happy and jump for joy, they want you happy, NOW!

Emotions cannot wait for you to figure things out; they operate as if your life depends on it. Sometimes, it does.

Sometimes, your emotions are mixed. You cry at a wedding, you laugh at misfortune. Mixed emotions are contradictions that can paralyze you.

You've learned that contradictions don't exist in the world. You've learned that contradictions are errors in thought or changes in context.

You've learned that humans create contradictions. They keep their contradictions and reject thinking. Your obligation to your mental health is to resolve your contradictions before they destroy you.

Our mission is nearly complete. You are arriving at the deepest level and the source of your power. You need to understand that although you can hold contradictions in your mind, unresolved contradictions are unhealthy. Contradictions form the ultimate box that blocks you.

14. The Source of Power—Your Mind in Harmony

Some people use mystical beliefs like God to define their source of power. That's fine if you realize that God is a myth—a mental symbol of excellence that you cherish and revere.

If you believe God is objectively real and created the universe, then you must prevent yourself from doubting. If you believe that God is simply a powerful myth that inspires you, then your doubt is no longer an issue. You, too, can learn what to do and how to do it to achieve mental harmony. It's your choice.

Before you can learn how to achieve mental harmony, you must understand that mental harmony is achievable *by you, from within you.* You must make that understanding your clear purpose.

The scene below is real. I was in my thirties when I got a powerful lesson about taking control. This lesson taught me the source of mental harmony. Once you know the source, we'll explore the characteristics of the mind that make mental harmony possible, achievable, and delightful.

Years ago, I was one of about 20 people in an adult driver training class. The instructor started the class by asking everyone to stand and close their eyes. Everyone obeyed.

He told us to put our hands behind our backs, the one hand close to the other, with both extended. He said, "Pretend that you're holding your hands so that someone could put handcuffs on you." There were some murmurs and sounds of surprise in the room.

"Ah, ha" he said after a pause. "You're not waiting to be handcuffed; you're standing on a sidewalk near the curb, waiting for a bus."

"Move your hands to the front of your body and extend them together like they're holding something that's pointing down," he continued. There were more murmurs and some shuffling sounds in the room. "Keep your eyes closed," he reminded.

"Oh, oh," he said. "It's starting to rain. There's no bus shelter here. What are you going to do? You're going to get wet…. No, you're not. You're holding an umbrella. That's what you have in your hands in front of you. Lift up your hands and open your umbrella. It's a beautiful, big, red umbrella and you can put it over your head. You can see that red umbrella in your mind's eye. You can take control."

I stood there thinking about the red umbrella in the rain.

"This class is about control," he said finally. "You can take control…. You can open your eyes and sit down."

Liftoff, this book, your mission, is about control. You can take control of your life. You can take control of your future. How? You must take control of your mind.

Each part of your mind has a unique function. In order to achieve mental harmony, your conscious mind must take control.

Your conscious mind leads and your subconscious follows.

When you get these two mixed up, the result is mental chaos.

When you learn something new, your conscious mind directs the learning. It asks the questions, makes the decisions, and guides the process. Your conscious mind decides why. It decides what's important and what's not important. It figures out stuff. It classifies stuff. It thinks. At least, on some level, the conscious mind is always the director of Job 1.

Your subconscious mind follows orders. It does what the conscious mind tells it to do to the limits of its ability. It stores stuff and retrieves it. The subconscious mind doesn't ask questions. It just comes back with right answers or wrong answers, and the conscious mind has to tell which is which. The clearer the instructions from the conscious mind, the more likely the answers will be what the conscious mind wants to get.

And here's the problem. If the conscious mind decides to accept a contradiction or, more exactly, not to resolve contradictions, instructions to the subconscious are likely to be vague. It's as if the conscious mind tells the subconscious, *"Just let it go. Don't make a big deal out of it. Store it somewhere. I'll think about it later."*

When you give your subconscious vague instructions, you leave it to your subconscious mind to figure out where the contradiction belongs. The subconscious cannot do that. It can only follow your conscious instructions to the best of its ability.

Because contradictions are errors in thought, they do not belong. If your instructions are not clear, your subconscious will be confused. Your mental storage will be messy. You will have mixed emotions. Your emotions are always calls for action. If your instructions to your subconscious are impossible because they depend on following contradictions, your subconscious will rebel. Your emotions may even give you nightmares.

Unresolved contradictions don't belong anywhere. If you have unresolved contradictions floating around in your mind, your subconscious doesn't know what to do.

When your conscious mind won't figure it out and your subconscious mind can't figure it out, what's left? Only emotions. Your emotions rule. They scream, "ACT NOW!"

If you're out of control, your emotions drive you to act whether the actions make sense or not. And whose fault is that?

It's always the fault of your leader and controller—your conscious mind.

So if you haven't gotten the message yet:

C'mon, _____, put on your big kid pants and take control.

Now I'm going to tell you what I did to solve the problem of contradictions when I took control. It's something I have never told anyone, ever. Some people may think it's the craziest thing they've ever heard, but I was desperate. It worked for me. Maybe you can figure out another way to deal with the contradictions you've accepted from childhood. I didn't.

When I was a teen, I discovered the danger of contradictions. Engaged at 18, I was floundering at 19. I was in college. I felt my future life was going to be a prison; my fiancé would be my jailor.

I desperately wanted freedom from my parents, but the price was very high. I wanted freedom and was about to accept "jail" to get freedom. The contradiction trapped me and paralyzed me until I broke my engagement.

Then I made a pledge to myself—and this is the amazing part because I didn't know anything about the subconscious mind or how it worked. I pledged to myself that I would never knowingly give myself a contradiction, but if I did, my subconscious should store it in a little locked room in the back of my mind.

The door should have a sign:

 DANGER

Contradictions here. Results unreliable.
Proceed at your own risk. Consider yourself warned.

I pledged that every once in a while, I would look at the contents of that room in the back of my mind. I would try to deal with them, one by one until the room was empty. I would do all the thinking necessary to put these strange, annoying contradictions to rest.

From then on, I had peace of mind. It wasn't always easy resolving the contradictions, but it was much easier than losing my strong feelings of positive energy and control.

Every so often, my subconscious would come back from a search empty handed. The answer was behind that dangerous locked door in the back of my mind. And yes, we had a consult.

"Here's the thing," my uppity subconscious would tell me, "We can't go there. One of us needs to figure out this contradiction. It's not going to be me."

Typically, my subconscious stored all the contradictions in one locked room. This turned out to be wonderful because sometimes when we opened the door, two contradictions locked in the same room were lying dead on the doorstep having cancelled each other out! I just had to kick them around a bit to make sure they were dead. Hallelujah!

If not, I would just have to take charge and whittle them down as much as I could.

THE PREQUEL TO THE JOB STACK STORY

I admit that my story about keeping a locked room in the back of my mind is bizarre. It deserves an example. There are no examples that I could give you that happened while I was a teen. I was as disorganized and confused as any typical teen.

I made my locked-room pledge somewhere around my twentieth birthday. I was an adult, and there was nothing I could do to change anything that went before.

However, the purpose of this book is to help you set out on the path to self-empowerment with an adult commitment. Perhaps the story I'm going to tell you now bears more on your situation than any that happened in my teenage years. My locked room pledge was my commitment to myself as an adult.

Life can be hard. There are pitfalls, dangers, and challenges. There are chances to succeed. Mental harmony is the most important gift you can give yourself, and you get mental harmony by attacking your inner contradictions and resolving them with clear thinking.

The best example I can give you of this process is the contradiction I didn't want to face the night my teenage son rescued me when I was overwhelmed. In fact, my entire adult career and view of myself were in chaos. In a way, this is the prequel to the Job Stack story in Chapter 2.

Previously, I had a big job at another company. A corporate takeover had ended that job. As a single mother with a son in private school and no help from my ex-husband, I couldn't afford to hold out for a job on a par with my experience. I started over at the bottom of a different corporate ladder.

I went from a job close to my town to commuting by train. My son's private school was 22 miles away. Moving wasn't an option. Busing wasn't an option.

I drove him 22 miles to school every day. Then I drove 11 more miles, parked my car, and caught a train to the city. If we were five minutes late leaving our house in the morning, I missed my train 33 miles away, and was late for work. I was late almost every day.

In the evenings, I did the reverse. My health deteriorated. I started getting asthma attacks around 3:00 a.m. every night. I couldn't walk from the train to the office without my inhaler. Until my son was old enough to drive to school, this was the commute from hell for both of us.

I had solid management experience from the first company. I worked hard and smart. I used my initiative to figure out what the company needed someone to do next and did it before anyone could ask.

I volunteered to take over a project that had stymied the new company for years. I had completed a similar project in the first company, so I knew just what to do and how to do it. Working on this new project, my asthma disappeared. My health improved.

I completed the project. The company promoted me. After five years of more projects and more successes, the company promoted me to group manager.

I was very proud of my big promotion. I was sure I could do the job and do it well. But reality told me otherwise. My group was floundering. My staff was overwhelmed.

The company had a work procedure. They were very strict about it since they said it served all the departments fairly. My group was required to process all requests for work in the order received. The principle we followed was "First In First Out," *no exceptions*.

The departments my staff supported needed special reports about their business. They weren't getting the reports they needed. They were frustrated and angry.

It seemed like I had six bosses, all wanting something different: my actual boss, his boss, and the four department heads. That's not even counting the dozens of analysts whom my group served.

They say that the squeaky wheel gets the grease. I felt like I was in a train wreck of squeaking and shrieking and the whole of my corporate life was crashing to a halt against an immovable mountain of warring priorities and needs.

My staff was demoralized and discouraged. It was a losing battle. I didn't want to admit that I was in over my head, but there it was. That was the contradiction I was hopelessly trying to avoid.

Part of me said, "Face it; you're losing the battle," and the other part of me said, "You cannot allow yourself to lose. Too much depends on it; too much is at stake."

By the time I got that promotion, my son was driving himself to school. So you can see, I was of two minds about my problem, and both sides of the question were about me.

Would I quit this job? Would they fire me? I told Gavin I felt like jumping out of a window, and perhaps that's when he really became concerned. Teenagers might think about jumping out of a window, not parents.

When Gavin said to me, "Mom, you've got it all backwards," I was very skeptical. What could he know; he was only 18! But when he started to speak, and I listened to his brilliant insight of how to organize work, I suddenly realized that the problem was not about me at all.

The contradiction was entirely in my own head. When I realized that the problem wasn't with me but with applying First In First Out to many jobs of radically different sizes and complexities, the contradiction disappeared.

Actually, they didn't quite disappear. When I went to the little locked room in the back of my mind and opened the door, there were the two warring sides of me, exhausted and battered, but arm in arm and smiling. There was no contradiction at all.

Of course, there were still going to be battles: the battle to get my group to follow my lead; the battle to get the company to change the procedure; the guerrilla war to wage to break the will of the other departments dedicated to First In First Out. All of those I could fight because my conscious mind and subconscious were working together. Wow, I was happy!

The only person I couldn't fight was myself, but now, between "me, myself, and I," we were all on the same side.

TAKING CONTROL

I cannot say that this crazy way is the only way. There's one easier way: never accept contradictions in the first place.

You can blame other people if you want, but that won't do you any good. You have to take responsibility. You have to take control of your life. You have to pledge to yourself that you want your subconscious on your side, not working against you. The only way you can do that is to give your subconscious orders that it can follow.

So your Job 1 in this chapter is to learn how to take control and stay in control.

The story of the locked room was one way my conscious mind took control. It gave the subconscious *standing orders* regarding contradictions. Standing orders are instructions that remain in effect until specifically changed.

Another way to think about the subconscious is that it is the part of your mind *responsible* for carrying out standing orders. These were the standing orders, "Put all contradictions in the locked-room. Don't let them out. Let me know if there's a problem."

You can give your subconscious standing orders for actions you have learned to do. The subconscious can do the job automatically with minimal supervision.

Some standing orders group a series of actions into a complete whole. When you first learned to tie your own shoes, it probably took you five minutes, and you had to think hard about each step to get it right. Now when you decide to put on your shoes and tie them, it seems like you don't have to think about it at all. You tie your shoes automatically.

Sometimes standing orders help you accomplish amazing things. When I was a teen, I had the job of washing the dinner dishes each night. At first I balked and complained, but after I learned how to do it, I could get all the dishes washed while I was thinking about other things.

One day, I was supposed to write a poem for English homework. What should I write? I had no clue. While I was doing the dishes, I zoned out. I started to think about how much I missed my grandmother who had died the previous year.

Suddenly, there were no more dishes to wash. My chore was completed. And just as suddenly, I knew exactly what I would write. I rushed into my room and wrote 14 lines of a sonnet in perfect rhyming form.

The words poured out of my head and on to the paper with no effort at all. I had two Job 1 assignments that night. The poem followed the dish washing effortlessly and without a break. Such are the benefits of standing orders.

When the conscious mind says, "Do it," your subconscious knows what do to. It does the job. Your conscious mind guides the process. If the process has many steps, the steps flow smoothly. Just think about how slowly you read when you first learned to read. Now the subconscious carries out the process automatically and gives your conscious mind the information. It's a brilliant system we humans have.

Of course, you must pay attention. Your conscious mind has to be alert to any irregularities in the process. When you're reading, you may need to look up words you don't know. When you're mowing the lawn, you don't want to run over a rock. When you're riding your bike, you don't want to hit a pedestrian or a fire hydrant.

What part of your mind gives the standing order? The only part of your mind that can give it, always and without exception, is your conscious mind, the part of your mind that takes control.

It should be clear by now that your subconscious is subordinate to your conscious mind. If they work together as they should, there will be harmony.

In emergency situations, if you've already practiced what to do, you're prepared to act. Your conscious mind knows what to do and your subconscious is prepared to carry out its orders. You can act quickly and save your life and the lives of people in danger.

If it's not an emergency, by now, you should know what part of your mind is in charge

There are only a few more things we need to say about the subconscious mind.

If you want to cross a room, you stand up and walk to the other side. What part of your mind sets your purpose? It's the only part of your mind that can set your purpose, always, and without exception. Your conscious mind is the part of your mind that takes control.

Standing orders can be more refined, and as you grew, you refined old standing orders. You knew how to eat in your high chair. Then you learned to how to feed yourself. Eventually, you fed yourself without dribbling. Then you learned to eat at the table.

You also refined what you like to eat and what you don't like. Throughout your life, you will give your subconscious new standing orders. You may learn how to drive a car, how to take a job or vacation. All of these will grow out of your observations of things and their characteristics in the world and your decisions about whether they are "for you" or "against you."

What part of your mind can change your standing orders or your purpose? Again, it's the only part of your mind that can give a standing order or set a purpose in the first place. Always and without exception, your conscious mind is the part of your mind that takes control.

Once you have a task or job done, it usually comes back, and you need to do it again. Practical life is like that. Brushing your teeth and making your bed are good examples.

When you first learned to brush your teeth, you had to think about each step. You put the toothpaste on the toothbrush. You learned the brushing strokes. You rinsed your mouth. You washed your brush. You put it away.

Now you don't even have to think about it. You may be thinking about something else entirely while you're brushing your teeth. You automate the action. Your subconscious guides your action based on standing orders you learned when you were a child.

For making your bed, you learned to smooth out the under sheet if it were bunched or pulled up. Then you learned that you needed to position and smooth the upper layers from bottom to top. Maybe you had the top sheet, the blanket, and the coverlet. If your pillow were in the way to do all of this, you moved it. When you had all the layers done, you put the pillow at the head of the bed. When you first learned to do this, it probably took you 5 minutes, but if you made it a habit, it may only take you a few seconds.

Why make it a habit? Making your bed is a very small accomplishment. However, at the end of the day, you get the small pleasure of seeing your bed made, knowing that a real grown-up sleeps there.

Early in this journey, you learned about the Job Stack. We said that Job 4 comes from the infinite world of jobs labeled 5. I promised to reveal how Job 5s make the Job Stack method a stupendous empowerment machine.

Every day, you run across Job 5s, the "don't even think about it" jobs. Your conscious mind notes that some may suit your purposes, but you are not ready to think about them.

I've already told you how I used my locked room to store contradictions, and I explored them and vanquished them as diligently as I could over the years. If new ones come up, I still use the locked room.

Now I'm going to tell you about the way I deal with Job 5s, the jobs I am not ready to think about. You can do it too.

When we have our purpose set, there will always be a world of Job 5s. We're too busy doing the jobs already on our plate. In the case of Job 5s, these are not contradictions that we don't know how to resolve; these are new opportunities for success.

As you experience many mini successes, your life purpose will become clear to you. With such clarity, you can hack through all the roadblocks to set yourself up for achievement without even knowing that you're doing it.

When you have a clear purpose, your conscious mind gives your subconscious clear standing orders. The clearer your purpose, the better your subconscious filing system.

When you run across an opportunity you're not ready to pursue, you know it's a Job 5. You have no time to think about it now.

You're too busy. Your subconscious just files everything related to your purpose.

When you've done Job 1, set up Job 2 and thought about Job 3, where will the new Job 4 come from? It will come from the Job 5s that your subconscious, obeying standing orders, organized by whatever criteria that matters most to you, and filed away.

When you're ready to pick your next Job 4 from the infinity of Job 5s, your subconscious goes first to your personal Job 5 "don't even think about it" stash. It retrieves the prospective Job 4s from your Job 5 stash, organized just the way that matters most to you. How powerful is that!

Will you ever run out of Job 5s? You run out of Job 5s when you fully satisfy your purpose. Then what do you do?

By now, you probably can guess:

C'mon, _____, put on your big kid pants and find a new purpose.

COMPLETING LEVEL III

Your mission in this book has been to understand how to power yourself from the kid you were to the adult you would most like to be.

Your mission in life, should you choose to embrace it, is to find your passion and spread the word on how your passion empowers you.

For some clues on how other people are working to fix the broken system, I encourage you to read the books suggested in *Further*

Reading for Teens and Young Adults. The authors there are inspiring heroes of self-empowerment. They inspired me.

From Don Watkins and Yaron Brook, comes an appropriate quote:

> "To live, each of us has to produce the material values our lives require, and the bulk of our time will be spent devoted to that task...What's important is that we constantly learn, grow, face, and overcome new challenges in a career that we love."[9]

Nearly every adult runs out of purpose at least once in a while. Now is not the time to falter or to stop. In the *Afterword* you will learn the final secret of self-empowerment: where to find your next purpose no matter how far you go.

I could have given you a review of Level III as I did with Levels I and II. But if you've really taken to *Liftoff*, I think you'll probably go back to re-read the chapters in Level III from time to time.

We're almost at the finish line. See you on the other side of the divide between kid and adult. It's no longer a big divide. Just go to the next page.

Afterword—Mission Accomplished

Hello and welcome.

Our mission together brought you here with the attitude, the tools, and the power to fuel your life's own adventure with a steady stream of successes that keep you excited about moving forward, enjoying the journey, and working toward an awesome destination.

At the beginning of this ride, you filled out your first negativity worksheet. If you've been working with *Liftoff* while you were reading, I hope you've had some satisfying successes.

People always say you need a purpose bigger than yourself. I say that too, but I say it with a difference. *I know you need to keep yourself instead of losing yourself.*

Of course, you need a purpose bigger than yourself. You're limited. You can't doubt that! The space between your ears is about 6 inches. For all practical purposes, the world, your world, is infinite.

The world should be your purpose. Survival in the world is the purpose of every living thing trying to stay alive. There's no reason for you as a creature of the world to have a purpose that's not of the world. The world is room enough.

Let the world be your purpose, and let your success be your guide to achieving an outstanding life.

Each success can lead to another. What do you like to do? What are you good at doing? What do you enjoy doing? Let your successes answer these questions. Your answers are your keys to your purpose and to your happiness. I can guarantee that if you find your purpose *in the world*, without losing yourself, you'll never run out of things to achieve.

What people pay you for doing empowers you to keep doing it! The source of your empowerment is your absolute conviction that you can do Job 1. You don't have to solve every problem of the universe. You don't have to do the jobs you don't know how to do. If you can do Job 1 and you know it, you are gold!

So go ahead and do it!

You cannot share empowerment by giving it away. You gain empowerment only by taking positive steps toward a goal. Make *Liftoff* part of your life. You will empower yourself because when you choose Job 1, it's the job you can do.

You may be asking, "Why teens?" Why me? This could be a book for everyone. My answer is that teens grow up and change the world. Teens are people just finding out that the system is broken. Adults have known that too, but it's a problem they cannot face.

LIFTOFF↗

Teens are the people still looking for the ideal adulthood for themselves.

When I was nineteen, I knew that the system was broken, but I thought someone else would fix it. I waited fifty years for someone else to fix it. Finally, I realized that it was up to me to show that if people individually could break out of the boxes that confine them, the system would not be broken. It would be working.

My purpose in writing this book was to empower you to empower yourself. You have a new life to live. You have new eyes to see the problems. You have a new mind to figure out solutions. With the book, you have a new method to see that the facts as the _characteristics of things_. You have a new will to change the world. You have young energy to do it.

And now, through _Liftoff_, you have three easy steps: do Job 1, set up Job 2, and think about Job 3. You know that Job 1 is the right job for you. You can apply _Liftoff_ to your life a little or a lot. You can use it all the time on paper or in your head.

Through _Liftoff_, you know how to hack your personal demons and flip them into positive actions. You know how to cultivate good habits and keep the Job Stack filled and flowing.

Best of all, you know how to kill those contradictions that plague and confuse you.

It may take you some time to make _Liftoff_ your own. You may not be able to automate the method right away. Be patient with yourself. You may need to use the worksheets for difficult goals. Paying attention to detail and practice will make the difference.

While you're underway, you can expand your knowledge by doing the worksheets and rereading some chapters. Keep growing to keep going.

Success is what you get by empowering yourself. Self-empowerment is what you get for yourself when you understand how others get self-empowerment from you by trading with you.

People acquire self-empowerment when they pay for the values they acquire.

As you learned from the short course in biology, all life requires action. Human life is different only in the fact that, unlike all other creatures, the human mode of survival is thinking. The product of thinking is human knowledge of the world. When people question and answer true limiting beliefs with facts, these facts become the basis of major advancements. Science creates new knowledge. Industry adapts the knowledge to new products. People are happy to trade their money for the comforts and longevity of modern life.

As a teen, armed with the right attitude and a practical method for getting things done, you have all you need to explore your strengths. You may not decide on a life plan right away. I advise you to decide to do every job to the best of your ability. Be determined to grow yourself into the best adult you can be.

When you find yourself in a paying job, respect yourself for doing it, and do it well. Remember, there are no lousy jobs, only lousy people who denigrate the value of honest work. If you believe in the goodness of your own honest work, then never be ashamed to collect a paycheck or make a profit on what you do.

Your paycheck or your profit empowers you to continue to live and thrive. You cannot work for nothing or take a loss and expect to thrive. A loss means spending more than you make, more than you profit. Losses transform you from powerful to powerless.

You can give your money away to your family, friends, or to charity. You can give money to strangers or people in need. You cannot give away success or self-empowerment. In fact, by giving money away, you actually rob people of the incentive to empower themselves.

Both success and self-empowerment must be earned. If you've read this far, done the worksheets, and started using the Job Stack, you've earned the self-empowerment you feel.

What can you do with your self-empowerment? You can decide to pursue a childhood dream. You can find a job that suits you well. You can write books, study law, medicine, science, or industry. You can make art or literature with a vision that thrills you.

Whatever you do, know that your self-empowerment, your expertise, and your love of your own ability to do Job 1 will see you through. Your career in your chosen field will empower others who pay you for your work.

If you want to fix the broken system, spread your empowerment and celebrate!

You're just beginning.

A Note to Parents

I have one hope to express to you.

I hope that *Liftoff* is the book you wish you had read when you were a teen. If it is, I want you to know it's not too late for you. There's always a Job 1 for you to do.

You can do it, or you can think about it. If you think about Jobs 1, 2, and 3 in the three easy steps, no matter where you are in your life, you can make your life better. If you make the three easy steps your habit, you can make your life better, much better. I encourage you to do that.

If you want to give this book to a teen, a teen important to you, do it *and stand away*. When your teen is ready for *Liftoff*, then *Liftoff* will be your teen's Job 1.

Appendix —Job 1 Log

Write what you would like to remember about the Job 1 that you did or tried to do. What was your purpose?

What did you want to accomplish and why? How did you do it? What did you learn?

If your life Purpose is known to you, write what it is and why. If your life Purpose is unknown (or only an inkling), write what you would like to explore and how you might like to explore those options.

Date: _____

Make every Job 1 outcome a learning experience.

_____

_____

_____

_____

_____

_____

_____

_____

_____

_____

_____

_____

_____

_____

_____

_____

_____

_____

_____

_____

_____

_____

_____

_____

_____

End Notes

1. An Interview with Thomas A. Edison," *New York World*, Mar 28, 1887, as quoted in the *Fort Myers Press*, Fort Myers, Florida, Apr 19, 1887. From http://edison.rutgers.edu/newsletter9.html. Accessed 1/28/16.

2. Bolt, Seth and Chandler. *Breaking Out of a Broken System*. p. CB-47.

3. Wikipedia. https://en.wikipedia.org/wiki/History_of_aviation. Accessed 1/28/16.

4. Wikipedia. https://en.wikipedia.org/wiki/Immanuel_Kant. Accessed 1/28/16.

5. Speicher, Betsy. *The WHYS Way to Success and Happiness*. p. 17.

6. American Heritage Dictionary.

7. InnerBody. http://www.innerbody.com/image/nerv02.html. Accessed 1/28/16.

8. Wikipedia. https://en.wikipedia.org/wiki/Membrane. Accessed 1/28/16.

9. Watkins, Don and Yaron Brook. *Equal is Unfair: America's Misguided Fight Against Income Inequality*. p. 58.

Further Reading for Teens and Young Adults

Allison, John A. *The Leadership Crisis and the Free Market Cure: Why the Future of Business Depends on the Return to Life, Liberty and the Pursuit of Happiness*. New York. McGraw-Hill Education. 2015.

Bolt, Seth & Chandler Bolt. *Breaking Out of a Broken System*. Summerville, SC. Bolt Bros. Publishing. 2014

Cushman, Charlotte. *Montessori: Why It Matters for Your Child's Success and Happiness*. Kerhonkson, NY. The Paper Tiger, Inc. 2014.

Epstein, Alexander J. *The Moral Case for Fossil Fuels*. New York. Portfolio/Penguin. 2014.

Rand, Ayn. *The Fountainhead*. New York. Plume. 1996.

Schaefer, Jack. *Shane*. New York. Bantam. 1983.

Speicher, Betsy. *The WHYS Way to Success and Happiness*. Westlake Village, CA. Sherman Oaks Press. 2015.

Watkins, Don and Yaron Brook. *Equal is Unfair: America's Misguided Fight Against Income Inequality*. St. Martin's Press. 2016.

Acknowledgements

Many fine people empowered me to bring this book to you.

I am grateful for the empowerment I received from Chandler Bolt and Self-Publishing School. I am grateful for the upbeat wisdom of my coach, Emily Rose. I am grateful for the *"you-can-do-it-NOW"* attitude of my accountability partner, Lori Chavez-Wysocki.

I am grateful to my friend, Dr. Susan Banta, who taught me her "deal with it" mantra.

I am grateful to my editors, Wayne Purdin and Fred Cookinham. Each made comments that motivated me to simplify and clarify the text. I am grateful to my awesome designer, Heidi Sutherlin. Her inspired design the captures the excitement, challenge and fun.

I am grateful to my mother, Ruth Bernstein, for my early training in figuring things out for myself. I am grateful to my father, Jacob Bear Bernstein, for his joy of living in the world.

I am grateful for the writings of Ayn Rand. I read *The Fountainhead* and *Atlas Shrugged*, when I was 19 and desperate. I have re-read both of these books many times. I am especially grateful for Rand's *Introduction to Objectivist Epistemology*, her stellar contribution to my thinking.

I am grateful to the Ayn Rand Institute (ARI) for its role of promoting Ayn Rand in the culture. I have met many fine people who advocate reason, purpose and self-esteem. In this book for teens, those three concepts form the basis of self-empowerment.

I add that ARI has not endorsed or sanctioned this book. At this writing, ARI is not aware of it. However, ARI continues to mean a great deal to me.

I am grateful to the other authors whom I recommend for further reading: John Allison, Yaron Brook, Don Watkins, Charlotte Cushman, Alexander J. Epstein and Betsy Speicher. Each is an inspiration shining the light of reason on a life passion.

I am grateful to my son, Gavin Skeen, whose key practical idea has guided my actions for many years and forms the core of this book. No one is more loving and giving.

Finally, I am grateful to Josh Huntington, my life partner and reward, who suffered stoically through my months of distraction, and who read and re-read the book, never wavering from his insistence on simplicity and clarity above all.

For the ideas expressed in this book and the ultimate manner of their expression, I take full responsibility.

Ilene Skeen
April 2016

About the Author

Ilene Skeen has had a passion for practical thinking since childhood. Her favorite pastimes were coloring books and jigsaw puzzles. These pastimes gave her thinking both a creative and analytical focus.

Ilene thought that becoming a grownup happened in kindergarten. She was astonished to learn that growing up would take thirteen years of school. She excelled in school except when she failed.

Later, in the business world, she called her early focus "creative problem solving." In her first job while in college, she devised a system that cut the weekly time spent on bank deposits from sixteen hours to two.

In 1974, Ilene discovered the opportunity in computers for her creative problem solving skills. She completed an MBA in Management and Operations Research, with distinction. She led projects in accounting, operations and planning.

Her largest project was a redesign the workflow that fed a computerized book printing plant. The new system reduced pre-press time to a tenth of the former system.

About the Author

In 2003, Ilene retired and earned an MA in Anthropology. She founded a website for artists in 2006, teaching herself the new computer languages and technologies.

In 2015, Ilene realized that practical thinking skills were rare and valuable. She decided to apply practical thinking to the most important problem everyone needs to solve: growing up.

Liftoff: The Self-Empowerment Guide for Teens is her first book.

Share Your Empowerment!

Thank you for reading my book! I really appreciate all of your feedback, and I love hearing what you have to say. Share your story or ask a question at http://liftoff4teens.com.

I'd love to hear about your empowerment and success, and so will other teens and adults. If you want to share your empowerment, write a helpful review on Amazon, your blog or social media.

Thanks so much!

14493601R00120

Printed in Poland
by Amazon Fulfillment
Poland Sp. z o.o., Wrocław